Symbol
Therapy

Symbol Therapy

Access your

Higher Consciousness

to solve your physical and

emotional problems

ULLI SPRINGETT

PIATKUS

✂ Visit the Piatkus website! ✂

Piatkus publishes a wide range of exciting fiction and non-fiction, including books on health, mind body & spirit, sex, self-help, cookery, biography and the paranormal. If you want to:

- read descriptions of our popular titles
- buy our books over the Internet
- take advantage of our special offers
- enter our monthly competition
- learn more about your favourite Piatkus authors

visit our website at:
www.piatkus.co.uk

Copyright © 2001 by Ulli Springett

First published in 2001 by
Judy Piatkus (Publishers) Limited
5 Windmill Street
London W1T 2JA
e-mail: info@piatkus.co.uk

The moral right of the author has been asserted

A catalogue record for this book is available from the British Library

ISBN 0 7499 2246 X

Text design by Zena Flax
Edited by John Malam

This book has been printed on paper manufactured with respect for the environment using wood from managed sustainable resources

Data manipulation by Phoenix Photosetting, Chatham
Printed and bound in Great Britain by Mackays of Chatham

Contents

Contents

Acknowledgements

FIRST OF ALL I want to thank all my Buddhist teachers, and in particular Rigdzin Shikpo. He guided me safely around all the pitfalls that lay on the spiritual path, and taught me about the true nature of the mind. Deepest thanks to Wally Sawford who is a very special Buddhist and Taoist teacher. He helped me to have meditation experiences which inspired me greatly. Thanks also to Barbara, Sue, Patrick, Christine, Daphne, John, Val, Pauline and Andrew, who shared and supported this process. I want to thank all my psychotherapeutic teachers, most of all Phyllis Krystal, from whom I learnt about the amazing effectiveness of symbols in the psychotherapeutic process. I am very grateful to my editor, Sandra Rigby, and to Judy Piatkus, for believing in me and my work. Thank you to all my clients who had the trust and the courage to try a new method and who shared their processes with me. Lots of thanks to Richard Sylvester, who enthusiastically explored all the possibilities of symbol therapy with me, and who generously copy-edited this book. Thanks to all my friends who believed in me and supported my work, in particular Jutta, Elke, Joy and Debby, and to my wonderful husband, Nigel, who readily tried symbol therapy as soon as I 'discovered' it, and who supported me in every respect. Without his generous help this book wouldn't have been written.

Introduction:
How did symbol therapy
come into existence?

FOUR YEARS AGO I had an experience that changed my life for ever. I was sitting in the shrine-room of my Buddhist teacher trying to listen to his talk. But I could not concentrate because I was inwardly struggling with an emotional problem which had accompanied me for most of my life. As I had often done before, I prayed deeply for help and – lo and behold! – this time my prayer was fulfilled. Suddenly, the method of symbol therapy 'popped' into my mind. It was so clear and elaborate that I assumed I had read it in a book and was just remembering it. In the months that followed I used this method to successfully solve my lifelong emotional problem, and many smaller issues as well.

I then introduced the method to my friends and family, and later to my clients. I carefully monitored their individual process and asked everybody to measure their success on a scale. The results were overwhelming.

Every single person who has used this method has had significant improvements with their problems. Symbol therapy seems to have the power to solve anybody's problems in a very straightforward way.

When I look back it seems as if a lot of my life had been leading up to this experience and had prepared me to 'receive' this method, refine it and, what's more, make it accessible to other people. Thirteen years ago I found Tibetan Buddhism like a lost child running into its mother's arms. It was a true experience of coming home, and I have never doubted for a second that I was on the best spiritual path available to me. From the very first day I had visited a Buddhist centre I meditated every day for at least an hour. I spent virtually all my holidays in intensive teaching and meditation retreats with knowledgeable and experienced teachers who guided me along the way. Over the years a deep motivation evolved in me: I wanted to develop so much happiness, insight and love that I could be of *real* benefit to other people.

A few years after I had started to meditate I began to work as a counsellor and psychotherapist and tried to put my desire to help other people into practice. I had completed several long-term psychotherapeutic train-ings, had gained qualifications and felt that my ability to help had grown considerably. However, I still felt a strong wish to find a psychotherapeutic technique that was much more effective in curing people than the one I was working with. I knew that my therapeutic methods were effective because I received positive feedback from both my clients and my colleagues. But in my opinion the results my clients were getting were too unreliable and the process took too long. In other words, the typical counselling process didn't suit my impatient nature. My ideal psychotherapeutic technique would be very simple. Everybody would be able to use it as a self-help tool and it would bring reliable, effective results every time it was used. In addition it should point people to the eternal truth that unconditioned happiness can only be found through spiritual development and the awakening of a loving heart.

When I 'discovered' symbol therapy I had no idea that it would fit this wish exactly in all its aspects. Only when one person after another had used the method, often with amazing results, did I become slowly convinced that I had been given a real gem.

The core of the practice is to make contact with your Higher Consciousness, which is the spiritual core of both yourself and the whole universe. People have given their Higher Consciousness many names. They call it God, the Goddess, the Buddha, or the Source. It is not important which name you choose or which spiritual path you follow. When using symbol therapy it doesn't make any difference. You can also perceive your Higher Consciousness simply as the part of your mind which is much more loving and wise than your everyday consciousness, the part which already knows the solution to all of your problems. For myself the Higher Consciousness is the enlightened mind personified in the form of beautiful enlightened beings.

For some people the presence and the working of their Higher Consciousness in their life is very obvious and wonderful, but for many people it isn't. Even if they are following a religious path they wonder why God doesn't seem to respond to their prayers, or why they can't overcome their psychological hang-ups despite a sincere meditation practice. When we are desperate and unhappy the whole universe seems to be devoid of any higher meaning or power.

The core of Higher Consciousness is altruistic love, a love that encompasses everything that exists. When we connect with our deep wish for love and open up to the possibility that more love can manifest in our life, the working of our Higher Consciousness becomes more obvious to us. I have seen it in my life, and in the life of everybody who has opened up to the love of their Higher Consciousness, like a flower to the sun. All that is needed is a childlike innocent wish to receive this love, and the trust that there is a Higher Power which can bring this love to us.

Most people's awareness of the presence of their Higher Consciousness grows slowly and quietly. Coming into closer contact with your Higher Consciousness is usually not an earth-shattering experience. It is more like a growing feeling of deep inner security, the knowledge that you are loved, and that there is the possibility of deep happiness in all of us.

Symbol therapy will help you to communicate with your Higher Consciousness and make its wisdom and love available in order to solve your personal problems. You will receive this help through the use of symbols. These symbols – when visualised regularly for just four minutes a day – have an amazing power to transform your problems. They can reach deep into your unconscious mind and put things right at the root of a problem. You don't even need to know all the intricate causes of your problem; symbol therapy is clearly solution-oriented. The practice is absolutely safe and you can achieve a significant decrease in your suffering with almost every problem in a matter of days or weeks. This may sound exaggerated – but it is true.

Ellen's results are a good example which demonstrate the sometimes stunning transformative power of symbol therapy. Ellen had been suffering from depression, social phobia and low self-esteem almost all her adult life. She had been in and out of psychotherapy, counselling and self-help groups for over fifteen years. Her depression was better when we met but she still suffered terribly from her social phobia and low self-esteem. I asked her to measure her suffering on a scale from zero to ten (zero is no suffering at all and ten is utter desperation) and she said she was at seven. This meant that she really was in pain. Ellen agreed to try symbol therapy out and I guided her into deep relaxation. She met her Higher Consciousness and received a healing-symbol in the form of a purple gem. Then I explained to her how she should visualise her symbol in the middle of her heart and breathe out its good qualities. However, Ellen was not very optimistic.

'*I don't expect instant results,*' she said, seriously.

'*Sure,*' I said. '*Just give it a go.*'

Two weeks later Ellen and I spoke on the phone.

'*I am one or two on the scale,*' she said, but she still wasn't very impressed. '*I definitely feel better,*' she told

5

me, *'but I can't believe it is the symbols. I probably feel better because it is the holiday.'*

'Just try it for another two weeks,' I said, smiling inwardly. I had known her reaction myself because sometimes the results of symbol therapy are too good to believe.

Two weeks later Ellen came to my practice. *'Ulli,'* she said, *'I am zero on the scale and I have never been zero before in all my life. The holiday is over and I have even had a terrible argument with my daughter's doctor. Normally that would have left me shattered. But I am still fine. I am cross with the doctor but happy with myself.'*

Of course, Ellen and I were both very pleased with her results. Ellen has remained well. Sometimes her old fears want to resurface but when she remembers her healing-symbol she can return to her positive state of mind in a very short time.

Most problems will change of their own accord when you do this practice but symbol therapy can also work as a catalyst. This means that visualising your healing-symbols may lead you to a person who will help you, to the discovery of a treatment that will cure your illness, or to a book that will explain to you the insights you need. Your whole life-situation can even change so that your initial problem disappears. On top of this you can use this technique to explore all aspects of your life and discover whether they are in alignment with your path towards the unfolding of your highest potential, which is your Higher Consciousness.

Symbol therapy is based on the principles of Buddhism, but the technique in itself is new and unique.

It can be used by anybody who feels inspired by it, and it will not interfere with the practice of any other treatment, belief system or religion.

At the time I 'discovered' symbol therapy I had been suffering for decades from a subtle but deep feeling of emotional hurt and sadness that seemed completely disconnected from what was actually going on in my life. This feeling would just not go away, no matter how much my life improved on the outer level and no matter how much I worked on my inner being with various psychotherapeutic methods and intensive Buddhist meditation. I had many wonderful experiences and spiritual insights during my meditations which strengthened my spiritual development, but the sadness returned, often after only a short while.

But despite this frustration something inside me told me that it was possible to solve my problem, just as I had solved many other problems in my life before. My life had improved in almost every respect and I had got rid of all my crippling neurotic symptoms. I had detached myself successfully from all the debilitating relationships which had brought me so much unhappiness. I had found my soul mate and our mutual spiritual practice seemed to open up the sky for us. I was doing work that I loved, I had good friends and everything was fine, except my old symptom of 'free-floating' sadness. This problem was such a hard nut to crack that I felt that if I could solve it I could heal myself and my clients of 'anything'. So I fervently wished that my suffering would not be in vain, but that I would be able to use my problem to discover the deepest principles of personal healing in order to help other people.

I feel that this wish has come true, and I am deeply grateful for it. I believe that my desire to use my own suffering in order to help others was one of the reasons that my prayer was answered by my 'discovering' symbol therapy. My pain has truly been like the grit in an oyster that has finally produced a beautiful precious pearl.

The first healing-symbol I received from my Higher Consciousness in order to overcome my suffering from this sadness was a round bush covered with large red flowers. I really did not know what it meant, but I visualised it every day and on every occasion that my sadness arose. It was really uncanny how the sadness was almost immediately reduced by more than half. I became more aware of how often I did things because I believed they were good for me even though I actually did not really like doing them. I also became aware of how often I tried to force things instead of trusting the natural flow and relaxing into it. Gradually, over the next months, I learnt to trust myself more and with the help of several different symbols which indicated how my process was deepening I grew much more able to relax into the depths of my being without interfering any more. With that, my lifelong sadness disappeared.

Working with symbols was not new to me because in my work as a psychotherapist I had been treating clients for years using the symbol-therapy developed by Phyllis Krystal. Her main symbol is designed to remove difficulties in relationships and it has always brought excellent results.

When I tried my own symbol therapy method on some of my other smaller issues I had very good results as well. Amazed and happy with this, I began to introduce my friends and family to the method. Invariably they had excellent results, too. During this time I refined the method into its final version using all the knowledge I had gained from my many years of training in Buddhism and transpersonal psychotherapy. Sometimes I had a strange feeling, as if an unseen force was guiding me in this process. For example, my own symptoms sometimes flared up for no clear reason and this caused me to read a certain book. The book didn't solve my problem but it gave me some important ideas which helped me to refine my own approach to symbol therapy. After I had made these improvements my symptoms disappeared as quickly as they had come. Over time symbol therapy brought me a degree of harmony, peace and happiness that I had never experienced before.

After my friends and I had experienced all these positive results I felt no hesitation in adding this practice to my psychotherapeutic repertoire when working with my clients.

Symbol therapy proved so effective that two things happened. Firstly, I dropped almost all my other techniques and methods in favour of symbol therapy. Secondly, the time my clients spent with me in therapy shortened drastically. Often they felt 'sorted out' after only a few sessions. In this time they had learnt the symbol therapy technique themselves and didn't need the help of a professional any more.

Using symbol therapy makes people much more independent. They do not need the help of a professional as much as before. This is because through symbol therapy they can quickly learn to rely on the help of their own Higher Consciousness. It is so straightforward that you can learn it from this book and practise it on your own or with the help of a friend.

—1—
Which problems can you solve with symbol therapy, and what kind of results can you expect?

*S*YMBOL THERAPY WAS DEVELOPED initially as a method of transpersonal psychotherapy, and it was intended to be used for emotional problems or relationship issues. But it has turned out that symbol therapy works equally well on other problems, such as financial worries, physical illnesses and spiritual blocks. Here are some typical problems you can tackle with symbol therapy:

- Anger and frustration
- Anxiety
- Being too dominant and controlling with others
- Compulsive behaviour
- Confusion
- Damage to your aura
- Depression
- Desperation

- Energy blocks
- Exhaustion, tiredness
- Feeling easily dominated and overwhelmed
- Feeling traumatised
- Feeling weighed down by responsibility
- Financial problems
- Frustration and problems to do with work
- Grief and hurt
- Guilt-feelings
- Lack of confidence
- Lack of direction in life
- Learning difficulties
- Loneliness, alienation
- Problems and stress in interpersonal relationships with others
- Problems in achieving what you want
- Problems in making decisions
- Psychic domination
- Physical illnesses
- Sadness
- Sexual problems
- Shock
- Spiritual confusion, spiritual blocks
- Stress
- Weight problems

Most people find that when they use this method their problems are solved exactly in the way they expected. But it is also important to be open to new and unexpected results. The solutions in symbol therapy come from your Higher Consciousness and its wisdom might direct you to a different kind of outcome than one you might have expected. This doesn't have to be a disappointment – sometimes you might even experience a little miracle. If you use symbol therapy correctly you will find that it will definitely reduce your suffering – in one way or another.

A client of mine, Val, had had extremely painful periods for more than twenty years. She had tried all kinds of treatment without any lasting success and had resigned herself to the fact that she had to take a handful of strong painkillers every month. Val felt really inspired by symbol therapy and started practising at once. When she got her next period she found to her amazement that her pain had reduced so much that she only needed one single painkiller. Encouraged by this success she carried on with her visualisation and in the following months she didn't need any painkillers at all. Val found this improvement amazing because she had never expected that it would be so easy.

Of course not every illness can be cured by doing symbol therapy on its own. But the practice can help you to find the right practitioner and the right treatment. Symbol therapy is not a replacement for any medical or psychiatric treatment, but it may greatly enhance the effects of good treatment.

Another client, Ron, tried symbol therapy because he had had problems in his relationship with his wife for a long time. They were not big problems – a lot of small niggles would be a good description – and their relationship had been chugging along without any significant highs or lows. When Ron tried symbol therapy he expected everything to simply get better. But, instead, something happened that was quite atypical for him. He suddenly felt an urge to sit down with his wife and really discuss all the little problems and irritations that had accumulated over the years – and this urge grew and grew. But talking about their problems was the very thing that Ron and his wife had avoided throughout their relationship. They had both always been afraid of it since they felt that any kind of argument might mean the end of their relationship. But to his astonishment, Ron noticed that his fear of discussing problems had significantly decreased. So he asked his wife to talk with him, and she agreed. Their conversation was not nearly as difficult as Ron had expected and they found compromises that worked much better than their usual silent, half-grudging arrangements.

Symbol therapy often has a positive effect on the people who are involved in your problem. Sometimes they change in ways you never thought possible. But it is important to note that this influence does not come from your personal mind with all its little egotistical concerns, but from your Higher Consciousness, which always works in the highest interest of everybody involved. This practice will lead you to a solution that will reduce the suffering of everybody involved in the way that is most healthy for you and the people around you. It is important to be open to the possibility of a new and unexpected outcome. The power of this practice will be greatly limited if you try to prescribe exactly how your problem should be solved or how other people should change.

As described in Ron's case, it is important to be actively involved in the process of symbol therapy. As well as visualising your healing-symbols you need to reflect on what you can do about your problem with all your intelligence and common sense. Your Higher Consciousness will help you and guide you in this process and the right ideas will come into your mind. But it is you who needs to follow these ideas up and put them into practice.

SUMMARY

• Symbol therapy can be used for almost any problem you are suffering from.

• It is important to be open to new and unexpected ways of solving your problem.

• You need to be actively involved in the process of symbol therapy and you need to put any ideas you have about how to solve your problem into practice.

• People who are involved in your problem might change in amazing ways, but it is not your personal will which brings about these changes. They are brought about by your Higher Consciousness, which always acts in the highest interest of everybody concerned.

—2—
Who can work with
symbol therapy?

THE BEST HELP ANYONE can offer is to give people an effective tool they can use to solve their problems themselves. Symbol therapy is such a tool. It is a self-help method designed for people who are interested in an effective way of solving their problems with a minimum of cost, time and energy. Basically, everybody who feels inspired by such a method can work with it.

I have observed, however, that not everybody wants to solve their problems in such a quick and effective way. In my psychotherapeutic practice I have experienced over and over again that people can be very attached to their problems. On the surface they maintain that they want to get better, but in reality they are much more interested in trying to convince me that their problem is insoluble. This attitude might seem peculiar because it seems like a contradiction for people to visit a psychotherapist but not really want to get better. But the truth (and the trouble) is that we all suffer to a certain extent from this condition. We all want to be really happy and healthy, but most of us are reluctant to radically question our way of life, let alone to really make changes which might feel uncomfortable to start with. We can't help this – it is how human beings are. Even if our attitudes and behaviour lead to us suffering, it is more important to most of us always to be proved right in what we do and believe than to admit our mistakes and make changes. Some people even feel rather offended if you tell them that there is a method that can get rid of their problems in a very short time and that their suffering doesn't need to be explored in depth and talked over for many hours. They react as if you want to take something which is very precious away from them. In some cases people have even felt sad after they have been very successful with symbol therapy. *'Why did I have to go through all those years of therapy, when it could have been so easy?'* they ask. *'What was that all about?'* I can't answer their questions other than sharing my feeling that symbol therapy is a wonderful gift that we just didn't receive earlier.

It is strange, but one cannot assume that everybody is ready to let go of their suffering. It seems to me that people need a certain amount of insight before they are ready for a method that offers radical changes quickly.

There are very few prerequisites for using symbol therapy. The first is that you need to have faith in your Higher Consciousness. You do not need to be spiritual or religious in order to use symbol therapy but you do need at least to trust that there is a part of you that is much more loving and wise than your everyday self. If you cannot believe that you have this wonderful part of yourself you can try pretending to believe it. In this way you can try symbol therapy out, and if it works you might develop a more genuine trust.

If you have religious or spiritual beliefs you might want to think of the central figure of your creed whenever your Higher Consciousness is mentioned. This might be God, the Goddess, the Virgin Mary, the Source, or the Buddha. Always see these figures surrounded by beautiful shimmering light. You don't need to add anything to your beliefs or take anything away from them. Symbol therapy will use the love, wisdom and strength of your religion or belief system in order to solve your personal problems for the highest good of all beings.

Another prerequisite for this practice is that you need to have the discipline and inner space to visualise the healing-symbol that you receive from your Higher Consciousness. It only takes two minutes twice a day and it can be done in most situations, such as while lying in bed or doing some housework.

Every two weeks you need half an hour of silence and relaxation to receive new symbols in case you need them. It is a good idea to tape the instructions for symbol therapy given in Chapter 23 and listen to them in a state of relaxation. Another possibility is to ask a friend to guide you through them. The instructions are given in such a way that most people find it very easy to visualise their Higher Consciousness and receive healing-symbols from it – even if they have never worked in this way before.

But there are always some people who claim that

they can't visualise. This 'problem' can easily be solved because the kind of visualisation you need to do in symbol therapy is so basic that anybody can do it. Here's how: look at a small object in front of you and study all the details. Now close your eyes and describe the object. If you can do this you can visualise enough to use symbol therapy effectively. You don't need to 'see' everything as clearly as if you were looking at it on the television. It is enough to have a certain sense of your symbol or to just 'know' what it looks like.

Some people are afraid to use therapeutic methods without the help of a professional therapist because they fear the method may bring up upsetting memories or a healing crisis (things get worse before they get better).

If you have these worries you can be reassured. Symbol therapy is safe and free of side-effects. One big advantage of this method is that it will never bring up distressing memories or upsetting material. It will lead you to the solution of your problem without a healing crisis and you will get all the necessary insights and help you need.

If you are already having treatment to solve a problem, symbol therapy will support and enhance its effects if it is the right treatment for you. But if there is a method that is more beneficial for you, symbol therapy will probably help you find out about it.

SUMMARY

• Symbol therapy is an effective self-help tool designed for people who are interested in solving their problems with a minimum of time, cost and energy.

• You need to have faith in your Higher Consciousness if you want to work with symbol therapy. You can view your Higher Consciousness as either the central figure of the spiritual path you follow or simply as the part of your mind that is more loving and wise than your everyday consciousness.

• You need to create the inner space to ask for your healing-symbols in deep relaxation and you need the discipline to work with your symbols for four minutes a day.

• Symbol therapy is a very straightforward method which is completely free of side-effects. Therefore it can usually be done without the help of a professional. No upsetting traumas from the past will come up and no healing crisis is to be expected.

—3—
How does symbol therapy work?

A CENTURY AGO *S*IGMUND *F*REUD developed his now famous model of the superego, the ego and the id. The conscious ego, Freud argued, struggles to keep the negative and antisocial drives of the id and the strict and limiting demands of the moralising superego at bay.

This model, and many of Freud's other theories, were hailed as great advances in understanding the human psyche. Most psychotherapies that were developed after Freud still use his basic ideas to explain how emotional disturbances come about and how they can be cured. Sadly, Freud's model of human nature leaves little hope for deep happiness and liberation because it does not recognise that there is a vast potential of positive qualities that lies within each of us and which is not part of his model.

Symbol therapy is based on a different model of the human mind, which basically has three parts:

- the conscious mind (also called the everyday or personal mind);
- the unconscious mind;
- the Higher Consciousness.

The conscious mind

Our conscious mind encompasses everything that we are aware of. This includes our sense perceptions, feelings, thoughts and memories. Although some of us like to think that the conscious mind is the largest part of the human mind, it is actually the smallest. It is like the tip of an iceberg that you see above the water, while the unconscious mind is the larger part beneath the waves.

The unconscious mind

The unconscious mind is many times bigger than the conscious mind. It contains all our experiences and perceptions in minute detail back to our birth and includes every detail of what we experienced in the womb. It even contains all the memories of our past lives. On top of this it contains everything we are experiencing at the moment but are not aware of. This may include background noises which we blank out in order to concentrate on what we are doing, or feelings and thoughts we don't want to deal with at the moment.

The unconscious mind is neither negative nor positive in itself. It is more like the store-room of our perceptions of all the internal and external experiences we have ever had.

Between the conscious and the unconscious mind is a semi-permeable boundary. Certain things which have been conscious become unconscious and certain things which have been forgotten can become conscious again. But, generally speaking, most of what is unconscious remains unconscious.

If you want to experience how things which have been unconscious become conscious you can try thinking about what you ate yesterday. And the day before yesterday. And the day before that. How far back can you remember? Probably not more than a few days. When you can't remember any further back the door between your conscious and unconscious mind has closed. This closed door between the conscious and unconscious mind is the major problem in every kind of psychotherapy that relies on recollecting old traumas in order to heal the patient. You can read more about this problem below, but first let me finish explaining this model of the human mind.

The Higher Consciousness

By far the biggest part of our mind is our Higher Consciousness because it permeates every other part of our mind and even goes beyond it. In fact, our Higher Consciousness is unlimited and permeates the entire universe, including the minds of every being. In this respect we cannot talk about our Higher Consciousness as something personal or individual. Our Higher Consciousness is something we share with every other being in the universe. It is outside of us and something other than what we think we are, yet it is also inside of us and is the core of our being. Most of us are unaware of the presence of our Higher Consciousness and it is the aim of every genuine spiritual path to make us fully in union with it.

It is difficult to imagine the vastness of our Higher Consciousness because it is more than our conscious mind can understand. Also, the notion that we all participate in an all-encompassing mind can seem like an insult to our personal mind, which wants to believe that we start and end where our body starts and ends, and that we are separate and highly individual beings.

No matter how hard we try to understand our Higher Consciousness we cannot fully grasp it. In order to accept its reality we need some faith because ultimately it is a mystery.

We come across the idea of something mysterious and all-encompassing in most religions. Christians call it the Holy Spirit or God, and Buddhists call it Buddha-nature. In this book I call it Higher Consciousness so that people of all religions or no religion can use it and work with it.

So what is our Higher Consciousness like?

Imagine for a moment that you feel utterly free, uplifted and without limitation. Nothing burdens you, no worries constrict you and joy fills your heart. You feel you have access to unlimited knowledge and infinite possibilities and you are able to do whatever you want. Now imagine that this vast space of freedom is filled with the sweetest and tenderest love flowing freely from your heart to all beings without discrimination. All notions of friends and enemies have gone; you can love everybody alike. You can see that people are suffering and the deepest compassion springs from your heart as you see them struggling. But you can also see the way to happiness with complete clarity and you realise that all the negative ways in which people behave come from their misguided search for happiness. You feel only one deep wish and that is to remove all the suffering that people are experiencing and show them the path to true happiness.

Can you imagine all this? These feelings and this wisdom will grow stronger as we develop towards more awareness of our Higher Consciousness. But our Higher Consciousness is more than I have just described – much more. The love, compassion and wisdom of our Higher Consciousness is infinite and without boundary. It truly goes beyond the limits of our imagination. Yet it is our true nature – it is what we ultimately are.

Sometimes we may have glimpses of our Higher Consciousness. But because we grasp at these experiences in order to control and prolong them, these short moments of bliss just remain glimpses. If we were able to rest in these moments of higher awareness, without the slightest notion of controlling or possessing them, our understanding of our Higher Consciousness would deepen.

So how can your Higher Consciousness help you to solve your problems? I have to go back a little bit to explain this.

You have probably noticed that many problems – in particular emotional problems – cannot be solved through merely thinking and talking about them. Of course it is valuable to talk in order to let off steam and get some sympathetic support, but this alone will not solve your problem if an essential part of it is unconscious. On the contrary, your problem can seem to get even bigger if you think and talk about it too much. It is like using a microscope and zooming in on your issue until nothing else exists – but still without finding a solution.

The same is true for health problems. You can wrack your brain and try to identify which psychological attitude or trauma might have caused your illness but in many cases this will not lead you to successfully curing your disease or ailment. The fact is that the root of your physical problem is probably unconscious and your analysis cannot touch it.

In order to solve problems like this we need to find a way to work effectively with the part in us that is causing the problem but is unconscious at the moment. One way of doing this is to enter psychotherapy, which tries to uncover unconscious material.

Several forms of psychotherapy work on the assumption that emotional or psychosomatic problems are caused by traumatic situations in the past. This past does not need to be just your childhood; it might also be the recent past or even your previous lives.

Typically therapists who practise these forms of psychotherapy believe that it is crucial to make this traumatic material conscious in order to release old negative feelings and to discover and correct any unhealthy decisions that someone has made at the time of the trauma.

Let me illustrate this with an example. A woman whose problem is that she cannot create committed and longstanding relationships enters psychotherapy. Through working with her unconscious mind she is regressed to the age of three and discovers that she was sexually abused. According to the theory she can now release her suppressed feelings of anger and grief. She can then correct any unhealthy attitudes that she has developed as a consequence of this trauma.

Different psychotherapies use different methods to regress the client and to make the unconscious conscious. Undoubtedly many people have benefited from this approach and still do, in particular when the regression is done in a gentle way and if there is a lot of emphasis on integrating the traumatic material. But bringing unconscious material to the light of day can have severe disadvantages as well. This is particularly true when the regression is done in a forceful way, as in therapies which use screaming and when the integration aspect is neglected.

The regression method in general doesn't acknowledge the fact that there is a very good reason why we have become unconscious of terrible traumas from the past. It is one of the most merciful qualities of our mind that it can forget the bad things of our past so readily. If you are more than thirty years old you have probably noticed that parts of your past seem better and better the older you become. This ability of our mind to forget so many of the bad things helps us to concentrate on our lives at the moment and to be free of many of the burdens of our past. People who cannot forget the traumas they have experienced suffer from post-traumatic stress, which can make their present life a living hell. They need help to actually forget the dreadful things of their past.

When we dig into our unconscious mind in order to release old traumas it can sometimes be utterly devastating. People who have discovered in psychotherapy that they were sexually abused as children have sometimes reported that their recollections were as distressing as if they had been sexually abused again. Instead of releasing old negative emotions they were swamped and overwhelmed by them.

It is very difficult to deal with recollections such as these. They can be extremely painful to bear and they can make you feel like a victim. To make matters even worse, there is no way of telling whether these 'memories' are true mirrors of reality. If we carefully investigate what is actually happening in any form of therapy that uncovers old traumas all we find are 'pictures in the mind'. Nobody can say for sure what these pictures really represent. Are they true recollections? Are they fantasies? Or a mixture of both?

Imagine that you discover in regression that you felt neglected as a baby. What do you do with this 'memory'? It is very difficult to go to your mother and ask her about it. In all likelihood she will be hurt by your questions and deny everything. But one thing is sure, it will make your relationship with her more difficult.

Fortunately, not everyone who has done regression therapy has experienced any of these negative side-effects. But symbol therapy offers a way to deal with the part of your problem that is unconscious in a way that is completely free of these risks. With symbol therapy you do not need to remember any traumas and you do not need to uncover anything that is distressing.

You might find it surprising but in order to overcome your problems you do not always need to understand their cause. It does not matter if the cause of a problem is related to your childhood or even from a past life. You do not need to know any of that.

All this searching for the cause of a problem is like the zooming-in process that was described above and it will make your problem appear bigger while not solving anything at all. Even if you find a cause for your problem it cannot be satisfactory because this cause will have yet another cause. And this earlier cause will have yet another cause. Looking for the cause of a problem can be interesting or even fascinating when you have a problem in which you are not involved emotionally. But if you are suffering, your analysis will not shorten the time of your suffering because you will still be as far away from the solution as before.

'*But how can I solve a problem if I don't even know its cause?*' you might ask.

Knowing the cause of a problem will not necessarily lead you to a solution. And it is the solution to the problem that we really need to find, not its cause!

This is where our Higher Consciousness comes into play. Because our Higher Consciousness penetrates your entire mind, including your unconscious, and because it is ultimately wise and loving it already knows the solutions to all of your problems. If we can access the wisdom of our Higher Consciousness we do not need to make unconscious material conscious. We can go for the solution straightaway. And, by the way, once we know the solution to our problem we often find that we have discovered its cause as well.

The big challenge at this point is how can we communicate with our Higher Consciousness. Most of us have only occasional glimpses of our Higher Consciousness. But if we are not really advanced practitioners of meditation, we have an unfortunate tendency to destroy these glimpses as soon as they arise because we grasp at them. However, there is a way to communicate with our Higher Consciousness even if we have never meditated before.

Language is not very suitable for this communication because it is always accompanied by the conceptual thought processes of our personal mind. These concepts, which are the basis of any thought, are often much too crude to communicate with higher forms of wisdom and compassion. What we need is something that will bridge the gap between our relatively crude personal mind and our Higher Consciousness. This bridge can be created with the help of symbols.

The idea of using symbols to communicate with our Higher Consciousness is not new. Most religions give us symbols to help us make this contact. The most important Christian symbol is Christ on the cross, and in Buddhism you find statues of Buddha which symbolise the enlightened mind.

Some forms of psychotherapy also use symbols. One very effective therapeutic method is described in Phyllis

Krystal's wonderful book *Cutting the Ties that Bind*. Psychosynthesis is another form of psychotherapy that uses symbols, but in a different way to symbol therapy.

Symbols are more than just little pictures or statues. They are charged with the energy and meaning of what they are meant to communicate and they really embody what they symbolise. So in effect the symbol and what the symbol stands for cannot be separated – they are one.

With symbols we can bridge three gaps. Firstly, we can make contact with our Higher Consciousness by using a symbol. Secondly, our Higher Consciousness can send messages back to us in the form of healing-symbols. Thirdly, we can focus on these healing-symbols in order to send messages deep into our unconscious mind. In our unconscious mind deep memories are usually stored in the form of pictures rather than in words. For this reason language does not work very well as a means of communicating with this part of our mind any more than with our Higher Consciousness. Using symbols is much more effective and will give your unconscious mind the information it needs to transform.

When we repeatedly give all parts of our mind a message from our Higher Consciousness in the form of a symbol we can achieve amazing results. New and healthy ideas arise, negative emotional patterns effortlessly decrease and our body starts to heal. We might also suddenly meet people who can help us, or we might find that our life circumstances begin to change mysteriously.

This process is safe, free of side-effects and most of all extremely effective. With symbol therapy you can work on problems which have their roots deep in your unconscious mind without getting the undesired side-effects of trying to uncover unconscious material.

'*Wait a minute,*' I can hear you saying, '*it can't be that easy! Surely you have to work with your problems at least a little bit?*'

You are right. You need to work with your problem – but not in a negative or self-destructive way. Unfortunately, many people think that self-development only works when there is a pain, crisis and suffering involved. This is not true; personal development can be completely free of pain – but only if you have the skilful means to achieve this. What you need is solution-oriented positive thinking that will create positive feelings, new possibilities and new insights.

Now, positive thinking is very popular, and for good reasons. Thinking positively is the key to feeling positive. Symbol therapy assumes that the root of all problems comes from having faulty beliefs about yourself, and about the world, and that the deepest cause of your suffering is your own core negative thought-patterns. Beliefs like 'I am not loveable' or 'women are not trustworthy' create certain energy-fields which cause negative emotions and bodily tensions which in turn can lead to neurotic or physical symptoms. Symbol therapy works on the level of these deep beliefs and it is only here that we can correct the root of our problems.

The trouble with positive thinking is that it works on the assumption that we can replace our negative beliefs simply by repeating as often as possible the opposite positive affirmation. Alas, it would be nice if it were so, but our negative beliefs will not go away that easily. On the contrary, if our beliefs are 'challenged' by repeated affirmations they can really put up a fight and they usually win. So, if you just *try to think* positive it can be a great effort. It can be a constant struggle to keep your inner negativity at bay and it can wear you out. You may even get on the nerves of your friends and family because they will quickly sense that your 'positiveness' is not really genuine. All you will get with this kind of phoney attitude is more self-denial and more separation from others which will lead you to feel even more frustrated and lonely.

The kind of positive thinking we need to solve our problems effectively must be more genuine. Rather than making an effort to think positively we merely need to open up to what is positive in ourselves and around us and really take it in. After all, our true nature and the true nature of the universe is Higher Consciousness, and this is positive in itself. No effort is needed to make it more positive. When you work with symbols you will come into closer contact with your Higher Consciousness and helpful and positive thoughts regarding your problem will occur naturally. You will not have to strain and make an effort to be positive.

After all this explanation you might still wonder how and why exactly symbol therapy brings about all these wonderful results. I have to admit that I don't have an answer to this. The deeper working principles of symbol therapy remain inexplicable like any other question that touches on the primordial ground of our being. The effectiveness of symbol therapy is like our Higher Consciousness itself – a mystery. So you need a little faith to give symbol therapy a serious try. Let's get started!

SUMMARY

• Our Higher Consciousness penetrates our entire unconscious mind and can change your problem at its root in mysterious ways. We don't even need to know the cause of our problem.

• In symbol therapy there is no risk of upsetting traumatic material coming to the surface as in many forms of therapy which work with regression.

• The way to communicate with our Higher Consciousness and our unconscious mind is through symbols rather than through words. Symbols are a more effective way to communicate with these parts of our mind.

• The healing-symbols given to you by your Higher Consciousness will help you to work with your problem in a constructive way and to think positively in a genuine way.

• Symbol therapy works on the level of the mind and on our deep-seated negative beliefs about reality. It is these erroneous and negative beliefs which cause all our problems.

−4−
Define your problem

*T*HE FIRST AND MOST IMPORTANT STEP is to define your problem precisely and correctly. In some cases this can be very easy, but in other cases the definition can be a challenge. However, because a lot of the success of symbol therapy hinges on properly defining your problem it is important to carry out this step carefully. If your definition of your problem is broad and vague the effects of symbol therapy will also be broad and vague. The more precisely you can point to the core of your problem the more effective symbol therapy will be.

Let's assume you are suffering from stress at work. It is not enough to define your problem simply as 'stress'. You need to pinpoint exactly what is making you stressed. Is the work itself too difficult? Is your boss too controlling? Do you have bitchy colleagues? Perhaps everything at your workplace is actually all right but you are suffering from low self-esteem and that is making you tense and insecure.

Let's say that you find the worst thing in your workplace is your controlling boss. You need to ask yourself what is the nature of your suffering with him. When we are suffering we *feel* something. You might feel pressurised or anxious or even humiliated by your boss. It is not the boss himself who is the problem. Your suffering comes from the way you relate to him in your *feelings*. So when you work with symbol therapy you need to address the negative feelings you have when you are experiencing your problem. In the example of stress in your workplace you might come to the conclusion that your worst problem is that you feel afraid of your boss.

Once you've defined your problem as precisely as this you can ask your Higher Consciousness for a healing-symbol to overcome your suffering from feeling afraid of your boss. When you have received this symbol you must work with it for two weeks. Later I will explain how you do this.

But first, let me give you another example of how to correctly define your problem. Perhaps you are one of the many people who suffer from being overweight and who would like to shed some pounds. It is not enough to define your problem as 'suffering from being overweight'. It is *the feeling about your weight* that causes you to suffer, not the weight itself. If you want to use symbol therapy for this problem you need to ask yourself: What exactly do I *feel* when I experience the suffering from being overweight? Do I feel frustrated? Ashamed?

Irritated? Or all three of these? Once you have pin-
pointed your feeling you can define your problem, for
example, as 'suffering from feeling frustrated and
ashamed because of my weight'.

Not everybody feels the same negative emotions
about the same problem. Some people may be depressed
about their weight and others really angry. (Some people
even like being overweight.) So when you use symbol
therapy you need to include in your definition the
disturbing *feelings* you have in conjunction with your
problem.

Sometimes it is easy to know what we feel. But if
you are like most people you will try to avoid feeling
your negative feelings as much as you can. Unfortunately this will make working with them and letting
them go more difficult. Here is a little exercise to help
you to name your negative feelings.

Pinpointing and naming your negative feeling

- All feelings and emotions happen at the interface
  of mind and body which means that they can be
  felt and sensed in both of them. It is much easier
  to experience the exact nature of your feelings
  when you focus on your body and when you feel
  the feelings as they appear to you in your
  physical body.
- Think of your problem and feel the suffering
  that it causes you.
- When you feel the negative feeling ask yourself:
  Where in my body do I feel this negative feeling?

- Don't worry if you can't answer this question immediately. Instead, scan your body in search of your negative feeling. Start with your toes. Is the negative feeling in your toes? In your feet? In your ankles, knees, thighs, abdomen, around the waist, in your chest, shoulders, arms, hands, neck, face or head?

Once you have found where your negative feeling is in your body ask yourself: What colour is this feeling? What is it made of? For example, you may experience sadness as a dark cloud in your chest, or anger as shiny steel-splinters in your abdomen.

- Ask yourself: If this feeling could make me do something what would it make me do? For example, grief might want you to curl up in a dark corner, or anger might want you to kick something.
- Once you have explored your feeling you can start to name it. You can try different names out until you find a word that fits best. Here is a list of feelings and emotions to choose from:

Addictive urges	Craving	Fatigue
Anger	Depression	Fear
Anxiety	Despair	Frustration
Apathy	Disgust	Greed
Bitterness	Embarrassment	Grief
Compulsion	Envy	Guilt
Confusion	Exhaustion	Hatred

Hopelessness	Obsession	Shyness
Humiliation	Rejection	Sorrow
Impatience	Remorse	Stress
Irritability	Resentment	Tiredness
Jealousy	Restlessness	Upset
Loneliness	Sadness	Worry
Melancholy	Shame	

• Once you have named your feeling you can relax
  and let the negative emotion subside. Then you
  can proceed with symbol therapy.

When you define your problem you can include two feelings in your definition, such as 'my suffering from
feeling angry and frustrated about the behaviour of my
mother-in-law'.

If you are suffering from a physical illness you can
name your problem as 'suffering from feeling pain' or
'suffering from feeling ill'. Pain or illness are obviously
not emotions, but defining your problem in this way will
work well.

When you define your problem don't try to guess
what the underlying or deeper problem might be. People
often come to me and say that they have this or that
symptom and then they start explaining to me all the
underlying causes to the extent that I start wondering
who the psychotherapist is – them or me. To use symbol
therapy you don't need all this 'psychologising'. In fact,
too much 'deep' analysis of your problem is not only
superfluous but makes things unnecessarily confusing.
For one thing we often don't know the underlying

reasons for our problems because they are stored safely away deep in our unconscious mind. Too much analysing is often no more than guesswork which makes the whole process vague again. To get the best results from symbol therapy you must always work with the most obvious problem and the feeling that is causing you the biggest suffering at the moment. The good news about this approach is that it is actually much easier than deeply analysing yourself.

When you have a problem which you know contains many aspects and layers (like divorce, for example) you should start with the most obvious general definition of your suffering and then work through the different layers with more specific symbols if they are still necessary. If you have such a multi-layered problem it is a good idea to read through Chapter 14 'Work through complex problems' before you proceed.

Sometimes people say that they are not suffering from any problem but that they have an unfulfilled wish. If only they had a partner or a job, they say, they would be happy. However, if you want to get the quick results which are promised at the beginning of this book you need to look at where you are suffering and define your problem accordingly. If you don't have a partner you might be suffering from feeling lonely or unfulfilled. If you don't have a job you might be suffering from feeling frustrated or worried. When you use symbol therapy for these problems you might not get the job or the partner you desire straightaway, but you will definitely feel better in a genuine way. And if you feel happier you will probably be more successful in your search for the something or someone you wish for.

If you don't feel any suffering and you want to focus mainly on making your wishes come true you can use symbol therapy as well. In Chapter 15 'Maximise your results', you can learn how you can do that. But please don't expect instant results. Making wishes come true can take a long time and you will need persistence and the right attitude. At the moment I am writing another book about all the fascinating possibilities of using symbols in order to make your wishes come true. The perspectives that this opens up are incredibly inspiring.

Symbol therapy is designed to remove your suffering and therefore you should label your problem in the following way:

> *'My suffering from feeling . . . '*
> *(name what you are suffering from as specifically as you can)*

Here are some examples of how to define your problem and how not to:

Correct definition of your problem	Incorrect
• *My suffering from feeling* afraid of my boss	• My suffering from my boss
• *My suffering from feeling* frustrated because of my weight	• My suffering from feeling fat ('fat' is not an emotion)

- *My suffering from feeling* lonely
- *My suffering from feeling* frustrated because I don't have enough money
- *My suffering from feeling* grief
- *My suffering from feeling* upset and angry because of arguments with my husband

- *My suffering from feeling* frustrated because I haven't found my dream job yet

- *My suffering from feeling* depressed
- *My suffering from feeling* the pain of sciatica

- My problem is that I have no girlfriend
- My suffering from having no money

- I want to be free of grief
- My suffering from my husband's temper (you need to discover *your own* emotion)

- I am suffering because I don't know which career to pursue
- Depression

- Sciatica

The reason why I am stressing the importance of defining your problem clearly is that an imprecise definition of a problem is often the cause when symbol therapy doesn't seem to be bringing the desired results. If you are not getting good results you must check to see whether you have defined your problem correctly.

One of my clients, John, had already worked successfully with symbol therapy for quite a while when he encountered a problem. He complained to me that his healing-symbol to overcome his suffering from low libido wasn't working at all. His libido, he said, hadn't increased the least bit. We looked at the definition of his problem a little bit more closely and sure enough we found that he hadn't defined it correctly. John was single at the time and greatly wished to find a partner. It wasn't his low libido at the moment that was bothering him. The real issue was that he *felt worried* that he might not perform sexually with a new girlfriend. So now he asked for a new healing-symbol, this time 'to overcome his suffering *from feeling worried* that he might not perform sexually with a new girlfriend'. When he worked with his new healing-symbol he got good results promptly.

SUMMARY

• You need to include in your definition the negative feeling you feel in the area of your problem.

• Define your problem in the following way: 'My suffering from feeling ...' (state here what you are suffering from).

—5—
Measure your suffering

*I*N THE NEXT STEP you need to measure how much you are suffering from your problem. After you have finished your first two weeks' period of symbol therapy you need to measure your suffering again and then you can compare the results. This quasi-scientific approach will give you precise feedback on how effective symbol therapy is and whether it really is working for you. Use the following scale to gauge the degree to which you are suffering.

Scale to measure your suffering

Zero   No suffering at all. At zero you don't have a problem.

One   You have a very slight problem which hardly bothers you at all.

Two   Your problem comes up every now and then. You can still ignore it most of the time.

Three   Your problem is hard to ignore any longer. You are still happy most of the time but you feel you have to do something to solve your problem.

Four   You have a problem you can't ignore any longer. You suffer a good deal, although you can still switch off from your problem sometimes.

Five   You really have a problem which involves you in a considerable amount of suffering.

Six   Switching off from your problem is becoming harder and harder. It bothers you most of the time and causes you a lot of suffering.

Seven   You have a big problem. You suffer most of the time and you feel an urgent need to remove this problem from your life.

Eight   You are really unhappy. You experience almost nothing except your suffering from your problem but you have a little hope left.

Nine   You are extremely unhappy. You are completely engulfed by your suffering with very few rare glimpses of hope.

Ten   You are completely and utterly desperate. You would scream in agony if you were allowed to. You are experiencing nothing but your suffering and you have no hope at all any more.

Measuring your suffering is something you come across in several forms of psychotherapy and it is a powerful tool. In symbol therapy it is useful mainly for two reasons. Firstly it gives you good feedback on the results of this method. We all have a tendency to quickly forget how much we were suffering in the past. Even after just the required initial period of two weeks of symbol therapy, you might already have forgotten how bad your problem was when you started. As a result you might not recognise the considerable improvement you have achieved. But if you see that symbol therapy is really effective it will enhance your trust in the practice and increase your motivation for carrying on with it. The following story illustrates this point.

Once I gave a talk on symbol therapy and at the end I guided everybody through the practice so that they could all try the method out. The whole group relaxed, made contact with their Higher Consciousness and received healing-symbols. Then I told everyone how to visualise their healing-symbol for the next two weeks.

One person who was at the talk phoned me two weeks later about something that had nothing to do with symbol therapy. After we had talked about this I asked her how she had got on with her healing-symbol. She told me that she had asked for a symbol to overcome her suffering from grief because her brother had recently died. She admitted, rather shyly, that she hadn't practised her healing-symbol for the required two-week period and that she had stopped as soon as she felt better. I reassured her that I didn't mind at all and asked her whether she could remember what her suffering had measured on the scale on the evening that I had given the talk. For a moment there was silence at the other end of the telephone. Then the woman said, *'Ulli, I can't believe that I was suffering so much. I had completely forgotten how bad it was only two weeks ago. When I was at your talk I felt my suffering measured eight on the scale – my whole life felt like it was one big trauma. I feel so much better now. I would say my suffering is no more than "three" on the scale.'*

There is a second reason for measuring your suffering. Let's assume you had a problem which measured six on the scale, which means that it was quite large. At the end of the first two week period you measure your suffering as four, which is still not very low but it's a full thirty per cent less than it was. If you are not using a scale you might conclude that symbol therapy isn't working for you because your problem hasn't disappeared completely. As a result you might give up on this method altogether. That would be very sad because another two-week period of symbol therapy with a new symbol might work on a deeper level of your problem. That could bring your suffering down to two, which would mean that you would then only be experiencing a very small amount of suffering.

Suppose that one or two on the scale is good enough for you and you decide to work on other more urgent areas of your life with symbol therapy. While you are doing this the suffering from your first problem stays more or less at two. Three months later you want to tackle your initial problem again and another two week period of symbol therapy brings your suffering down to one or even less. Now you have overcome your problem completely. It is much easier to work on your problems in this disciplined and consistent way if you can monitor your process precisely and from this derive your motivation for keeping going.

Some people don't like to measure their suffering on a scale. They find it difficult to think about their emotions in numbers. This is understandable because our emotions come from the right half of our brain and our ability to think logically in numbers comes from the left hemisphere of our brain. It is not always easy to get the two hemispheres to work together.

However, the more the halves of our brain are in harmony the more effective and successful we can be as a whole being. Then we don't need to have different compartments for our emotional, intuitive and creative concepts on the one hand and our rational, analytical and logical concepts on the other. Instead, we are able to respond to every situation both emotionally and rationally at the same time.

Using numbers to measure our suffering is a way of training ourselves to bring our two hemispheres more into harmony. It brings rational awareness to more emotional people and emotional awareness to people who are more analytical and rational.

SUMMARY

• Measure how much you are suffering on a scale from zero to ten (zero is no suffering at all and ten is utter desperation).

• Measure your suffering again after you have done symbol therapy for two weeks and compare the results.

• Having this clear feedback about the positive effects of symbol therapy will enhance your motivation and stamina and encourage you to carry on with it.

• Measuring your suffering can help to bring the two hemispheres of your brain more into harmony.

—6—
Relax deeply

ONCE YOU HAVE DEFINED your problem and you have measured your suffering we can start in earnest. You need to get in contact with your Higher Consciousness so that you can ask for a healing-symbol to overcome your suffering from your particular problem.

Our Higher Consciousness is the core of our being, our true nature and the true nature of the whole universe. Yet we are rarely fully in contact with it. Somebody who is truly at one with their Higher Consciousness has transcended the human world – yet nobody will be more human than this person. They will be more humble and more compassionate than anybody else. They will be full of inspiring humour and have the deep wisdom to help others. Our Higher Consciousness is the crown of human development and the way we transcend it at the same time.

Why is it so difficult to get more into contact with our Higher Consciousness? If it is our true nature, why can't we be more aware of it?

The biggest hindrance to recognising our Higher Consciousness is fear. This is a very deep and basic fear which we all carry around with us even if we are not aware of it. It is this fear that motivates most of our thoughts and actions and fuels our constant questions such as: How can I get what I want? Am I being supported? How can I get rid of the things I don't like? How can I stop myself being invaded and controlled by others?

We might not be very conscious of these questions, nor of the fear that lies behind them. Yet they control how most of us tackle most of the situations in our life.

When we are in complete union with our Higher Consciousness all these questions cease to exist. In a state of unity with our Higher Consciousness we are completely free of fear and completely trusting. There is nothing but a constant flow of love and joy and the natural wisdom which enables us to do whatever is beneficial for everybody. What happens to us is no longer the most important thing any more, not because it is virtuous to be like that but because we don't need to be concerned about ourselves the whole time. Somebody who is in contact with their Higher Consciousness is so happy that they have energy and genuine concern for others, naturally and effortlessly.

When we have fewer fears and we are more genuinely trusting we become more aware of our Higher Consciousness and we develop more real confidence in ourselves. This is not the same confidence we see in arrogant and self-centred people. True confidence makes our heart open and compassionate and makes us very modest in a happy way. When we lose our basic fears we don't need to think about ourselves constantly. It genuinely doesn't matter so much how we look, how much money we earn and what others think of us. We are just too happy to be bothered by issues such as these.

The challenge is how to overcome our deep fears and get closer to our Higher Consciousness.

The best antidote to fear is relaxation. It is physically and psychologically impossible to experience fear in a relaxed body and mind. It would be a contradiction to do so because fear is nothing other than tension. You have probably noticed how tense your body becomes when you are really afraid, how your breathing becomes fast and shallow and how your mind can't stop thinking about the very thing that is making you afraid. If you could lie down, relax your whole body, practise deep breathing and let go of the stressful inner images, your anxiety would disappear within minutes.

Relaxation is used in virtually all the world's mystical traditions in order to bring people into closer contact with their Higher Consciousness. Every meditation starts with deep relaxation and practices such as the repetition of prayers or mantras have the same relaxing effect on the mind. In order to experience our Higher Consciousness we need at least for a short while to let go of our fear-arousing and ego-centred questions about how to get what we want and how to get rid of what we don't want. These questions are not bad in themselves. We need them in order to function in the world. But they do get in the way when we want to be in contact with our Higher Consciousness. The more relaxed we are and the more we can switch off the usual chatter in our mind, the more we can get in touch with our Higher Consciousness and receive the symbols which will solve our problems effectively. And once we've made this reliable connection with our Higher Consciousness we will be happier because it will be easier to let go of our fearful self-concern.

For some people relaxation is very easy because they have practised it for a long time. For others it can be a new and challenging endeavour. Some people have a relaxed body but a very tense mind, and other people have a relaxed body and a sleepy mind. Neither state is desirable for symbol therapy. The ideal we are aiming at is a relaxed body and a calm but alert mind.

If you have practised relaxation exercises before you can use whatever relaxation method suits you best for symbol therapy. In Chapter 22, The complete practice of symbol therapy, you will find a reliable and effective method of relaxation. If you find that this form of relaxation doesn't work for you, here are two alternative methods.

RELAXATION METHOD A

- Sit or lie down comfortably and undo any belts or tight clothing.
- Let yourself become aware of the rhythm of your breathing without altering it. Imagine you

are sitting on a sledge and every time you breathe out you are sliding down a sunny, snowy mountain-slope. Your sledge comes to a gentle standstill as your outbreath finishes. Be aware of the short gap before you find yourself breathing in. Breathe in and as you breathe out see yourself sliding down the gentle mountain-slope once more. Carry on breathing like this for a few moments.

- Tense the muscles in your feet as you breathe in and when you breathe out release all the tension in your feet. Tense the muscles of your calves and then release them with your next outbreath. Continue in this way and tense and then release the muscles of your thighs, stomach, chest, shoulders, arms, hands, neck, face and head.
- Imagine you are sitting on a beautiful cloud and you are sailing gently towards a wonderful place of your choosing, such as a beach or a garden. When you have arrived at this beautiful place climb down off your cloud and sit or lie down somewhere where you feel comfortable.
- Enjoy your deep relaxation.

RELAXATION METHOD B

- Sit or lie down comfortably and undo any belts or tight clothing.
- Feel your right leg becoming more and more relaxed. Feel your left leg becoming more and more relaxed. Your right arm becomes more and

more relaxed and so does your left arm. Your
whole body becomes more and more relaxed.
- Now your right leg becomes comfortably warm.
Your left leg becomes comfortably warm. Your
right arm becomes comfortably warm and so
does your left arm. Finally your whole body
becomes comfortably warm.
- See yourself drifting through an endless open
space. You feel wonderful in this space. You are
surrounded by love and happiness and you feel
free and liberated.
- Now you see a beautiful bright light in the
distance. You feel drawn to this light and you
move nearer and nearer to it. Finally, you enter
the radiant light and it surrounds you with pure
love. You merge with this light and then you
move through it. When you've passed through
the light you find yourself in a beautiful place. It
might be a garden or a beach or a beautiful
house.
- In this beautiful place, find somewhere to sit or
lie down comfortably.
- Enjoy your deep relaxation.

SUMMARY

- The biggest obstacle to making contact with your
Higher Consciousness is the basic fear everybody
carries around with them.

- A relaxed body and a calm but alert mind will help us

to let go of our fears and experience more of our Higher Consciousness.

• Nobody is more humble and human than someone who is genuinely in contact with their Higher Consciousness.

–7–
Open up to your Higher Consciousness

*O*NCE *YOU ARE RELAXED*, your usual worries and tensions will have decreased and the channel to your Higher Consciousness will be more open. Everybody can open up to their Higher Consciousness and create a more powerful connection. There is only one condition for doing this and that is that you have to ask for it. The higher powers of the universe are always there to help us, but they can only do so if we ask them.

Opening up to your Higher Consciousness will probably not be very difficult for you if you pray regularly as part of your spiritual path. You can simply visualise or sense the central figure of your religion and open your heart to them. It is not necessary to see an image of your Higher Consciousness. It is more important to have a feeling of deep trust that it is really there and cares for you.

If you do not have a religion or spiritual path you might see your Higher Consciousness in a more personalised form. It may appear to you in the form of an angelic being or as a wise old man.

But one word of caution – your Higher Consciousness may appear to you in many forms, but this doesn't mean that it is yours in the sense that you 'own' a personal Higher Consciousness. Nobody really has their own personal Higher Consciousness. We all share our Higher Consciousness because it is the nature of the universe and we are a natural part of it.

For many people their Higher Consciousness appears effortlessly to their inner eye. If your Higher Consciousness doesn't appear spontaneously to you, you can choose how you want to imagine it. Many people like to perceive their Higher Consciousness simply as a shimmering light that has a living and loving quality.

You might ask how Higher Consciousness can take all these different forms. The answer is that we always perceive our Higher Consciousness from our personal point of view. We all live in different contexts which are determined by our culture, our belief system, our upbringing and our religious schooling. This personal context determines both the way we perceive the world and the way we perceive our Higher Consciousness. There is nothing wrong with this because our Higher Consciousness isn't bothered about how we perceive it. From its point of view it is only important that we open up to it.

In whatever form you perceive your Higher Consciousness, two things are important: your Higher

Consciousness is always wise and loving, and it is never critical and judgmental. If your Higher Consciousness seems to be criticising you or anybody else, you must realise that the channel to your Higher Consciousness is blocked. The critical voice that you hear is actually the voice of your own personal consciousness.

'But how can I know that I am perceiving my Higher Consciousness correctly and that I am not making it up?' you might ask.

The answer to this question is – 'don't worry'. For symbol therapy to work you don't need to perceive your Higher Consciousness in a kind of mystical vision. You only need to be ready and willing to open up to it. When we do open up most of us will perceive a mixture of our Higher Consciousness and our own personal consciousness. On a 'good day' we will perceive more of our Higher Consciousness and less of our personal mind, and on a 'less good day' we will perceive more of ourselves and less of our Higher Consciousness. This is absolutely normal and does not decrease the effectiveness of symbol therapy. To use symbol therapy you don't need to be an advanced spiritual seeker. You simply need to have some openness and some faith in your Higher Consciousness.

However, if you notice that your Higher Consciousness doesn't appear loving and wise to you but instead seems judgmental or critical, you need to go deeply into relaxation and ask once more to contact your Higher Consciousness.

Your next question is probably this: *'How can I expect to get an effective healing-symbol from my Higher*

Consciousness if I am likely to confuse it with my personal consciousness?'

The answer to this is faith and repetition. All religions work through faith and repetition and we do the same in symbol therapy. You repeat your healing-symbol over a period of two weeks while maintaining your faith in your Higher Consciousness. In this way your healing-symbol becomes more and more charged with the power of your Higher Consciousness. Even if your symbol has come partly from your personal consciousness it will become more and more powerful through the repetition of your visualisation and through faith. The whole question of whether or not you are making up your Higher Consciousness and the healing-symbols will become irrelevant. At the end of the day the only thing that matters is whether symbol therapy helps you or not.

Once you are more in contact with your Higher Consciousness you have a short dialogue with it. You need to ask your Higher Consciousness for help and you need to be open to whatever it gives to you.

Asking for help can be difficult for some of us because it means admitting that we can't solve everything ourselves and that we are not as strong and self-reliant as we would like to be. But in order to gain the full benefit of the help of our Higher Consciousness we have to give up the notion that we are a 'self-made' man or woman. We are not completely autonomous and not completely in control. Giving up these illusions can be a real blow to our idea of who and what we are.

'But isn't our Higher Consciousness a part of our-selves?' someone might ask.

Yes, our Higher Consciousness is a part of ourselves but paradoxically it is also somebody else. When we ask for help we need to perceive our Higher Consciousness as something higher and stronger than ourselves. If we think our Higher Consciousness is just an extended part of ourselves we can't really open up to its enormous power. The help of our Higher Consciousness is the most beautiful gift we can receive and we need openness and modesty to receive it gratefully.

SUMMARY

• You have to open up to your Higher Consciousness in order to contact it more closely and you have to ask for its help in order to receive this help.

• You can choose the way you want to perceive your Higher Consciousness but you can't 'own' it in a personal way. We always share our Higher Consciousness with all beings in the universe.

• Your Higher Consciousness is always wise and loving. If it seems judgmental or critical you are actually perceiving your personal consciousness. In this case you need to relax and to tune in again.

• Faith and repetition will charge your healing-symbol with the power of your Higher Consciousness so that any question you may have about whether you are making everything up yourself becomes irrelevant.

—8—
Explore your
life-path

IN THE NEXT STEP you can discover the impact your
problem is having on your life-path towards your
deepest fulfilment. It will also give you clues about how
to make your journey go more smoothly and faster.

At first you have to imagine that your Higher
Consciousness is sitting on top of a mountain. As we
discussed before you don't need to 'see' a clear picture
when you visualise this. It is enough to have an idea of
the mountain and of your Higher Consciousness.

Now you have to ask your Higher Consciousness to
show you a road, a path or a track leading up the
mountain towards the top. This road symbolises your
life-path. This is your individual path towards your
highest unfoldment.

We all lead different kinds of lives. One person is a
computer consultant and another is a teacher or a house-
wife. Whether the life we have chosen makes us truly

happy or not depends on one fact alone and that is whether it brings us nearer to our Higher Consciousness. In our picture this journey is symbolised by the road that leads towards our Higher Consciousness on top of the mountain.

There are as many different roads towards Higher Consciousness as there are beings. Nobody needs to develop in exactly the same way as anybody else, either personally or spiritually. We are all free to find the path that exactly suits our needs and talents. This is why a life as a businessman can be as valuable from a spiritual point of view as a life as a monk. It is not what we are doing that is the most important factor. What counts is our *motivation* for doing it.

Developing towards our Higher Consciousness means realising the natural love and compassion for all beings that is dormant within us. It means becoming truly and deeply happy and gaining the liberating wisdom which teaches us the true nature of the universe and of ourselves. And it means helping others to realise the happiness we've found for ourselves.

Different people see their life-path in very different ways. For some it is a wide paved road and for others it is a steep rocky path. Most people see their life-path as having different sections representing the different phases in their life which are more or less difficult.

Once you have received an answer from your Higher Consciousness you need to thank it. It is not that our Higher Consciousness needs this 'thank you'. It is simply good for yourself. Every time you acknowledge the help you receive you become more open and receptive. And the more open you are the more you will get the full benefit of this work.

The next step is to ask your Higher Consciousness to show you where you are on your life-path. You might get a picture or an idea of yourself standing down in the valley, or you might see yourself already near the top. It really doesn't matter where you are on your life-path. What matters is whether or not you are moving forward. You will get a sense of where you are moving as you ask this question more often over time. Whenever we behave more egotistically or aggressively we move backwards on the path. Whenever we slide into more ignorance through using drugs or through addictive behaviour we also move backwards. And whenever we ignore our true needs and talents and try to adapt ourselves to situations which aren't really serving our development, once again we move backwards. To move forward on the path we need to become more confident, loving and compassionate, we need to gain more wisdom and we need to become genuinely happier.

In what way will you receive answers from your Higher Consciousness and how can you be sure that they are genuine? Unfortunately there is not much that distinguishes messages from your Higher Consciousness from your own thought processes. These messages may come into your mind as thoughts, pictures, feelings or body sensations. Even if the pictures and ideas you receive feel great there is no guarantee that they are genuinely and exclusively channelled from your Higher Consciousness. Some people claim that they get a certain body sensation as a sign when their Higher Consciousness is actually speaking to them. These claims are questionable. If it was that easy to make pure and clear contact with our Higher Consciousness without confusing it with our personal consciousness most spiritual seekers would probably be enlightened very quickly. The truth is that it needs the dedication of a lifetime and the constant refinement of our own personal consciousness to merge with our Higher Consciousness. Signs that we are doing so are feelings of beauty, love and meaning.

It is important to be realistic about this in order not to fall into the trap of a spiritual ego-trip. People who claim to have greater spiritual experiences than is actually the case are not doing themselves a favour. In fact, there is not much that will hinder their progress and development more because boasting destroys all other efforts on the spiritual path. If there is one sign of a truly realised being it is their deep and genuine humility.

So take whatever comes into your mind with a pinch of salt and see if it makes sense to you. What matters is whether you can learn something from the answer and whether it serves your development. An answer from your Higher Consciousness that helps you has two qualities. It feels true and it brings some feeling of relief. This sense of relief is a very good sign that your contact with your Higher Consciousness is deepening. Even if you get an answer that you don't really like, if it is true it will still bring some sense of relief because a part of us always feels relieved when we are confronted with the truth.

For most people it is fairly simple to see the road that leads to their Higher Consciousness and to get an idea of where they are standing on it. But sometimes people get a feeling that the image they have received doesn't make sense. They feel that it is their own fantasy or even pure nonsense. If you feel like this you can ask your Higher Consciousness again. If you still don't get a meaningful answer you can go back to your relaxation and try again a little later. You might then get another inner picture that feels more 'right' to you or you might get the same picture as before. In that case you can ask whether this picture really comes from your Higher Consciousness. Watch out for an inner feeling of 'yes', a feeling of relief or relaxation, or for a deep outbreath. These are all signs that you are on the right track. If you feel unhappy with your answer, or tense or awkward, it is very likely that your inner image has come from your personal consciousness and you will have to try again.

If you check your answers in this way with your Higher Consciousness you shouldn't do it more than two or three times. The part of your mind that receives answers on an intuitive level tires quickly and it is better to give yourself a break after two or three attempts if you don't get a response that feels right.

When you have practised symbol therapy for some time your intuition about the truthfulness of your inner answers will deepen. As with any other skill it is a matter of practice. What is important is that you do not give up too soon.

Sometimes people say that they don't get a response at all when they ask their Higher Consciousness a question. In most cases this isn't true. Many people actually do get an inner picture or thought but they quickly dismiss it. Then they wait for another idea but this doesn't work. It can't work because by dismissing what came first they have shifted their state of consciousness and are now less connected to their Higher Consciousness.

If you find that you are not getting an answer from your Higher Consciousness check to see whether you dismissed the first thought that came into your mind after you asked your question. If you find that this is the case you can ask your Higher Consciousness if your first thought was the right answer or whether you can have another message. In this way you will be able to stay in contact with your Higher Consciousness.

Occasionally people are not relaxed enough to receive an answer from their Higher Consciousness. In this case they need to choose a more appropriate time to relax and try again.

The first time I asked to be shown my life-path I saw a huge mountain. It had a rocky slope near the top which only an experienced rock-climber would be able to climb. In the middle there was a steep stony path and near the bottom it had a fairly flat wide road. I saw myself on this road down in the valley. I was pleased with this image because I liked the prospect of a flat easy road for a while.

Explore your problem

Your life-path represents the path of your personal and spiritual growth and it shows you the shortest and the best way to develop your full potential. Think about what would be a perfect way for you to learn a new language. Would you like to take an intensive language course, or would you like to spend a long time in the foreign country? We are all different and what works for one person might not work for another. This is as true for learning a new language as it is for developing your personal and spiritual potential. Not everybody can develop best by being a social worker, for example, nor is everybody lucky enough to be in good health and the freedom that goes with that.

There may be several different roads leading to our Higher Consciousness and we have many choices about which one we follow. However, one path is the shortest and this path will bring us the deepest happiness. If we can find this path we will be most fulfilled in whatever we do.

Nobody has set this path out for us. It simply is the path that unfolds our full potential in the best way. We are completely free to follow our life-path or not. This means we can decide for ourselves whether we want to grow personally and spiritually. Nothing and nobody can force us to develop our potential. Not even our Higher Consciousness can do that. Only we ourselves can develop the motivation and understanding to learn from both the good and the bad things that happen in our lives.

When this learning process is going smoothly and happily we are following our life-path – the path that leads directly to our Higher Consciousness. The most difficult lessons in our life are about how to deal with major disappointments and traumas. To move quickly along our life-path we need to develop a compassionate heart and a discerning mind no matter what is happening to us. If we fail to do that and become bitter or depressed, or allow ourselves to be controlled by others, life becomes hard and our progress on our life-path is slow. We might even find ourselves walking back down the path.

The obvious question that follows is: *'How can I know whether I am following my life-path?'* The answer is that the happier we are in what we are doing, and the happier we are in our relationships, the more likely it is that we are following our life-path. When we unfold our greatest talents and pursue our deepest wishes we are at our happiest. When we relate to other people in a way that most serves our mutual needs this brings happiness as well. And from this basis of abundance we are able to serve others in the most effective way possible. This service to others is what ultimately determines whether we move closer to our Higher Consciousness or not. The kind of service we are talking about here comes effortlessly from the natural wish to give, rather than from a strained effort to be a virtuous person. When you pursue your greatest talents and wishes, and when you feel satisfied in your relationships, you are most likely to be able to give in this naturally selfless and generous way.

If we have a problem which is causing us a lot of suffering it means that we are not following our life-path completely. On our life-path there are no problems – only challenges which we are happy to overcome. On our life-path we may experience adversity but we will not suffer much because we know how to turn problems into wisdom and compassion. For example, if we are rejected by our family, following our life-path means using this situation to develop extraordinary personal strength instead of becoming bitter and depressed. If we are seriously ill, following our life-path means finding a way to use this illness for personal growth instead of becoming resentful about it. Whenever we experience a lot of negative feelings we are straying in one way or another from our life-path.

But please don't think that suffering is something bad or a sign that you are failing in your development. On the contrary, for most of us suffering is the only thing that will turn us again and again towards a concern for our inner growth. Without suffering most of us wouldn't ever dream of following a path of self-development involving effort and discipline. Only through recognising our suffering and admitting to it can we use it to progress along our life-path more happily.

So, in the next question we ask our Higher Consciousness what we are doing on our life-path when we are experiencing the suffering from our specific problem. When we experience negative feelings and suffering we are not walking happily on our life-path. At best we might be walking slowly and with effort. But we are more likely to be standing still, sitting down, moving backwards or even moving along other paths which lead us away from our Higher Consciousness. It is best to ask this question in the following way:

> **'Higher Consciousness, can you please show me what I am doing on my life-path when I suffer from feeling ... '**
> (name what you are suffering from as specifically as you can)

Peter suffered from worries about money. When he asked his Higher Consciousness what he was doing on his life-path when he was suffering from feeling worried he saw himself crouching down and feeling tense.

Another client, Claire, suffered from a major problem in her relationship with her boyfriend. When she asked her Higher Consciousness what she was doing on her life-path when she was experiencing this problem she saw herself walking along a different path that led away from her Higher Consciousness.

Most people readily get inner pictures or ideas when they ask this question and these pictures often make immediate sense to them. When we are confronted with the truth it is as if something clicks into place. The picture you receive may give you an initial idea about how to solve your problem although you don't need to be able to interpret it in a detailed way. Pictures are like clues and can give you a general idea of what is going on. For example, Claire, with her problem with her boyfriend, doesn't need to know exactly what it means when she sees herself walking along a path that leads away from her Higher Consciousness. She only needs to know that her problem is so severe that she has strayed from her life-path altogether. If she carries on in the same way she will become more and more unhappy because she is moving further away from her Higher Consciousness instead of nearer to it.

Again, it is important not to judge yourself if you find that you are not walking happily along your life-path. Instead, see this information as the first step to improving your life. After all, if you don't know that you've lost your life-path you can't do anything to find it again.

Clarify your life-path further

There are many more ways to explore your life-path but these are not a necessary part of the symbol therapy method. For example, you can ask your Higher Consciousness questions about how to develop more love, compassion, wisdom and happiness. In this way you can receive guidance which will help you to make decisions in all areas of your life.

One client of mine, David, wanted to change his career. David felt that he could move in any of three different directions and because he felt very uncertain about what he should do he decided to consult his Higher Consciousness. After he had relaxed he asked his Higher Consciousness to show him his life-path and the place where he was at the moment. He received an answer to his question quite easily. Then in turn he asked what he would be doing on his life-path if he pursued each of his three different career options. He got the following answers. When he asked about starting his own business, he saw himself moving hectically up and down his life-path. When he interpreted this answer later it was clear to him that he wouldn't make any real progress in moving closer to his Higher Consciousness if he started his own business. David felt that this hectic up and down movement symbolised the stress he would be under and he knew that this wouldn't help his development. His second career option was to go back to his old teaching profession. When he asked his Higher Consciousness what he would be doing on his life-path if he went back to his old job he got an immediate picture of himself sliding down the mountain. This answer was clear – if he went back to his old job he would go backwards rather than forwards.

His third option was counselling. When he asked his Higher Consciousness about this he saw himself walking up his life-path, but it seemed a rather strenuous climb. This option seemed to be more in harmony with his life-path but David felt that he wanted a job that was less strenuous. For the time being we had to leave it there.

Like many people, David was concerned about whether the answers he got were true. Maybe, he said, he was just making these answers up in accordance with his own wishes and beliefs. I told him that this was possible but not very likely. In order to prove my point I asked him to ask his Higher Consciousness again and then to try to make his pictures up himself. The crucial point, I said, is whether the pictures will stay stable when he is relaxed. Ideas that come from the Higher Consciousness will feel relaxing and bring a sense of relief and they don't need any inner effort to be maintained. David did what I suggested and discovered that it was really difficult to change his inner images by his own will-power. He tried hard to imagine himself on other parts of his life-path but it didn't work very well. As if by magic he saw himself moving back into the position his Higher Consciousness had shown him before.

Many people who work regularly with symbol therapy and the life-path questions share David's experience. The inner pictures and ideas they receive from their Higher Consciousness seem to have a growing strength of their own and they are difficult to change. In other words, it is not so easy to lie to yourself when using this method.

My friend Karen found this out when she decided to check whether any of her relationships were out of alignment with her life-path. It shocked her a bit to discover that one of her closest friendships was actually causing her to go backwards on her life-path. (Thankfully this friend wasn't me!)

Karen thought about this picture carefully and finally admitted to herself that she had felt more and more uncomfortable with this friendship for the past two years. She realised that she had tried to ignore these negative feelings because she was quite attached to her friend. Karen was confronted through this work with a truth she had successfully blocked out. However, once she was over her initial shock she knew that the answer from her Higher Consciousness was right.

Karen certainly didn't want to break up with her friend. But resolving the conflicts she had with her would be difficult as well. Karen decided to work with symbol therapy and asked for a symbol to overcome her suffering in her relationship with her friend. Through this practice and the resulting insights Karen gained more inner distance from her friend and felt much better. She still loved her friend but she stopped being attached to her in an unhealthy way.

With the life-path questions you can ask your Higher Consciousness about the different options that are open to you. You can also test whether your relationships are serving your highest development and you can check whether specific areas of your life are in harmony with your Higher Consciousness or not. Here is a list of questions you can ask:

Higher Consciousness what am I doing on my life-path when I:

- do a certain job?
- am in a certain relationship?
- am pursuing a certain hobby?
- follow a particular spiritual direction or teacher?
- am in a certain kind of psychotherapy?
- relate to my mother/father girlfriend/boyfriend daughter/son in a certain way?
- pursue a certain wish?
- move to a certain town/area/house?
- spend my days in a certain way?

Of course, this list is not exhaustive and you can add whatever questions are relevant to your life.

Although it is difficult to lie to yourself with this method you mustn't take the answers you get as unshakeable truth. Whatever you receive, you need to use your common sense to check it because your own biases, wishes and concepts may still be bound up with it. This is particularly true if you have just started to work with symbol therapy. If you are having a bad day, for example, the answers that you receive could be tainted by your pessimism.

But, generally speaking, the very fact that you are

trying to develop more contact with your Higher Consciousness will make the answers more reliable. If you make it a habit to check your decisions regularly using this method you will find that you will develop a new and wonderful certainty about what is good for you and the people around you.

Unfortunately there is one question we can't ask and that is: *'What* should *I do on my life-path?'* It would be great if we could get straightforward answers to this question. But, unfortunately, this doesn't work. In order to live a life that is moving in the direction of our highest unfoldment we have to do most of the work ourselves. We have to think, feel and decide for ourselves what would be the appropriate steps to take and then we have to present our Higher Consciousness with the different options. We need to ask whether each option is in harmony with our life-path and then we can receive inner images which will help us to decide which direction to go in.

'Do we have to obey these inner images and follow whatever they tell us?' somebody might ask. The answer is 'no'. Symbol therapy is not a method that tells you what to do. At the end of the day it is you and only you who has full responsibility for whatever you do. You will always need to use all your intelligence and common sense to make the right decisions. What symbol therapy does is to offer you a method to improve your access to your intuitive inner wisdom. The beauty of symbol therapy is that people who haven't had much experience in this field before can gain reliable access to the wisdom of their Higher Consciousness.

Sometimes people are shocked to discover that what they are doing doesn't seem to be in harmony with their life-path. They think that they are failing because they are not developing in the best way they are capable of. The opposite is true! Human development works mainly through trial and error. Unfortunately, there is no one who can tell us what we should always do in order to develop our full potential. It is mainly through recognising our errors that we can progress. This act of recognition demands a great deal of courage and dedication to our self-development. When we discover we have made a mistake we should not feel depressed. On the contrary, we should celebrate our discovery. Only through recognising our errors will we be able to take the appropriate steps that will enable us to develop towards more happiness and fulfilment.

SUMMARY

• Your life-path is the path of your own personal and spiritual development and it leads towards your Higher Consciousness. It is your choice whether you follow it or not.

• Ask your Higher Consciousness to show you where you are on your life-path at the moment.

• Messages from your Higher Consciousness come into your mind as thoughts, feelings, images or body-sensations. If you are not sure whether you have received a genuine message from your Higher

Consciousness you can ask again. Feelings of relief, beauty and meaning are signs that you are on the right track.

• In order to move forward on your life-path, you need to develop more love, happiness and understanding in whatever you have chosen to do.

• When we are walking along our life-path we don't experience a lot of suffering because we can quickly use our problems to develop wisdom and compassion. When we are suffering a lot it is a sign that we are straying from our life-path.

• Ask your Higher Consciousness: 'Can you please show me what I am doing on my life-path when I suffer from feeling (name the problem)?'

• You can work with symbol therapy to bring every part of your life into alignment with your development towards your Higher Consciousness.

—9—
Ask for your healing-symbol

*N*OW *WE COME TO* the heart of symbol therapy practice. After you have explored your problem with the life-path questions you can ask for a healing-symbol to overcome the suffering your problem is causing you. It is important to ask for your healing-symbol in the following specific way:

> **'Higher Consciousness** *(or whatever name you call it)*, **can you please give me a healing-symbol to overcome my suffering from feeling** ... *(name the problem)* **for the highest good of all beings.'**

Someone suffering from depression might ask in this way: *'Dear God, can you please give me a healing-symbol to overcome my suffering from feeling depressed for the highest good of all beings.'* She should not ask: *'Dear God, can I please have a symbol for more joy in life for the high-est good of all beings.'*

There is nothing wrong in asking for a symbol for a positive aim, as in the second example. But if you ask your question in this way you will often find that you won't get the reliable quick results that are promised at the beginning of this book. If you ask for a symbol for a specific positive aim, rather than just asking openly for a symbol to overcome your suffering, there will be fewer ways in which your Higher Consciousness can solve your problem. It can therefore take much longer to solve it. But when you are completely open to whatever way your Higher Consciousness wants to help, it can work much faster and the whole process will be much more effective.

Imagine a man who feels that he hasn't got enough money. (I know that this will be an extremely rare case!) If he asks for a healing-symbol to overcome his suffer-ing from feeling frustrated from not having enough money, his Higher Consciousness can help in exactly the way that is needed. Maybe he will be guided towards finding a job which brings him more money. But not everybody who feels that they haven't got enough money actually needs more money. Maybe the man in our example needs to learn to spend his money more wisely. In that case his Higher Consciousness might send him a person who can teach him just that. Or he might suddenly realise that his wish for more money is a substitute for the wish for spiritual fulfil-ment. In that case he can ask for a new healing-symbol to overcome his suffering from feeling dissatisfied because of lack of spiritual fulfilment. In this way he can work on a deeper level of his initial problem.

As I was writing this a friend phoned me and told me about the latest results of his symbol therapy. My friend had retired early and, like the man in our example, he had worried a lot about money and about how he could survive on his small pension as he gets older. Sometimes these worries had been so bad that he had felt panic-stricken. Two months ago he had decided to use symbol therapy to solve this problem. He measured his suffering as a seven on the scale and asked for a healing-symbol. After practising with it for several days a chain of unlikely coincidences put him in the house of friends of a friend in his favourite seaside town. They had a lovely afternoon together and chatted about many things. One topic was house prices and my friend learnt to his astonishment that house prices in this seaside town were only half as much as in the town where he lived. In a flash he realised that this could solve all his money problems. If he sold the house he lived in at the moment he could not only move to his favourite seaside town but he would have enough money for his old age. My friend has been at zero on the scale of money worries ever since.

Your Higher Consciousness will know better than anybody else – including yourself – what is good for you at any given moment. Don't limit the way your Higher Consciousness can help you by telling it what to do. It is much more effective to be open to whatever solution your Higher Consciousness comes up with.

Let me give you a more drastic example. If somebody has a fatal illness it is unlikely that symbol therapy
will cure them. But if they can open up to the wisdom of
their Higher Consciousness the final months of their life
can be filled with enormous blessings.

Even if we can't always have exactly what we want,
we always have the choice of moving towards our Higher
Consciousness no matter how difficult our situation is.
And this spiritual development will ultimately deter-
mine whether we are happy or not. Here are some more
examples of correct and incorrect ways of asking for
your healing-symbols:

Correct
'Dear Buddha, can you please give me a healing-
symbol to overcome my suffering from feeling upset
about the constant arguments with my partner for the
highest good of all beings.'

Incorrect
'Dear Buddha, can you please give me a healing-
symbol for more harmony between my partner and
me.'

Correct
'Primordial source, can you please give me a healing-
symbol to overcome my suffering from the pain in my
stomach for the highest good of all beings.'

Incorrect
'Primordial source, can you please give me a healing-
symbol for good health for the good of all beings.'

Why is it so important to always add the phrase 'for the highest good of all beings'? It is necessary to say these words each time you ask for a healing-symbol and to really mean it because it makes it more likely that you will receive help from your Higher Consciousness. Our Higher Consciousness is the expression of absolute love and compassion and it is the complete opposite of any kind of selfishness. Egotism, which means wishing good only for ourself and not caring about others, is what separates us from our Higher Consciousness. To counteract any conscious or hidden egotistical tendencies it is important to really want the solution of your problem to be for the highest good of *all* beings. With this selfless motivation you narrow the gap between yourself and your Higher Consciousness and that makes it more likely that you will receive its help. It is not that your Higher Consciousness doesn't want to help you if you are selfish. But somebody who is in a very egotistical state of mind is simply not very open to their Higher Consciousness. They are not on the same wavelength, so to speak.

When people ask for their healing-symbol most of them have an instant thought or picture coming into their mind. It is important not to miss it because it may occur within a split-second. People can very easily dismiss this first image and afterwards their mind seems to be blocked. To avoid this, try to acknowledge whatever comes into your mind.

Don't take a particular healing-symbol that is shown to you if you don't really like it. As I said earlier, there is always the possibility that your own ideas and concepts have interfered with the process. It is important that you like your healing-symbol and that you feel good about it. If you don't like your symbol and you have a resistance to it, it won't be able to enter deep into your unconscious mind and do the transformative work that is necessary. Your healing-symbol needs to be positive, meaningful and pleasing. A symbol that looks ugly, boring and negative to you cannot represent the solution to your problem.

If you receive a healing-symbol that doesn't feel good to you for whatever reason, you need to ask your Higher Consciousness for another one. Don't take a symbol you feel ambivalent about and don't try to change the symbol yourself. If you are not sure whether a specific symbol is the right one for you, you can ask your Higher Consciousness for confirmation. An inner 'yes' or a feeling of relief and relaxation are signs that this healing-symbol will work for you. If you don't get an inner feeling of confirmation look out for an inner feeling of 'no'. If you don't feel any resistance against your symbol you are most likely on the right track as well.

I once had a client who found it very difficult to throw anything away, so her apartment was filled with an incredible amount of stuff. She received a pink axe as a healing-symbol, which seemed appropriate at first glance. But I was suspicious. Usually our Higher Consciousness doesn't give us such 'aggressive' symbols. So I asked my client how she felt about her healing-symbol and sure enough she said she felt ambivalent. I suggested that she ask for a more pleasant symbol and in the end she got a pink heart, which helped her a lot.

But one word of caution. If you haven't received a healing-symbol after three or four tries give yourself a break and try again later. The part of your mind that can receive information on an intuitive level can tire quickly – particularly when you don't use it very often. Your personal consciousness will partially come back and interfere with the process. This is especially true if you become impatient or frustrated.

For the same reasons don't ask your Higher Consciousness for confirmation more than once after you have received either a symbol or any other information. If you ask more often your focus can easily shift and once this has happened you won't be able to receive answers from your Higher Consciousness any more for the time being.

But don't worry – you don't need to have a 'perfect' healing-symbol in order to get the best results from symbol therapy. Even if your personal mind has interfered in the process (which is very likely) you can make up for this by practising your healing-symbol regularly and through having faith in your Higher Consciousness. Your faith will charge your healing-symbol more and more with the power of your Higher Consciousness and the practice of symbol therapy will work beautifully.

Sometimes people have difficulty in 'seeing' their healing-symbol clearly. It can appear vague and fragmented to them. This doesn't need to be a problem either. Even if you don't see your symbol clearly you probably have an idea of how it would look if you could see it. Just ask your Higher Consciousness if you have received the right idea and check for an inner feeling of confirmation. If you get an inner feeling of 'yes' (or at least not a 'no') you can go on and work with this healing-symbol. Don't worry if it continues to appear unclear. It is enough for you to 'know' how it looks.

There is a multitude of possibilities for the kind of healing-symbol you might get. You might see geometrical shapes, animals, plants, stones, places, or different kinds of people and scenery.

As I have already said, you don't need to see or to sense every detail of the symbol you receive. And you don't need to be able to interpret its meaning. But two things are important – you need to see or at least know both the colour and the shape of the healing-symbol. The colour is particularly important. If you have heard about healing with colours and light you probably know that different colours have different healing-qualities and that they are successfully used to cure emotional and physical problems. The best known colour therapy is probably the one that is used to treat jaundice in newborns. Every colour carries a certain vibration and it is this vibration that brings the transformative information which will improve your problem. Surprisingly, it doesn't seem to matter whether we are experiencing 'real' coloured light or whether we are just imagining it. The healing-process works in either case. So when we do symbol therapy we need to use healing-symbols with a bright and beautiful colour. If you receive a symbol which is black or has a dull colour, or which has no colour at all, you need to ask your Higher Consciousness for a beautiful bright colour.

If you know a lot about colour-healing it is good to forget your knowledge about which colour is meant to cure which problem when you ask for your healing-symbol. Try to be as open as you can and allow yourself to be surprised by the colour your Higher Consciousness shows you. What matters is that you *like* your symbol.

Some people have difficulties perceiving colours with their inner eye. If this is the case for you, you need to find out whether the colour is being 'shown' to you in other ways. Maybe the word 'pink' flickers through your mind. Or you might think of grass without seeing its colour directly. In this case you'll know that your healing-symbol is green.

Here is a list of what you can you do if you have difficulties in receiving a healing-symbol:

- Check whether you have dismissed the first thought that came into your mind after asking for your healing-symbol. If that is the case ask your Higher Consciousness if your first thought was the right healing-symbol.
- Maybe you expected to 'see' a symbol but instead you 'heard' an idea for a symbol. Maybe you even 'felt' a symbol. Check whether you have received a symbol through a different channel than you expected.
- Maybe you weren't relaxed enough to receive a symbol. Go back to your relaxation and try again a little later.

- Try to make your request for a symbol to your Higher Consciousness with more passion. Really mean it!
- Before you ask for your healing-symbol picture a lake. When you make your request to your Higher Consciousness see a symbol emerging from the middle of the lake.
- Before you ask for your healing-symbol picture the dark night sky. When you make your request to your Higher Consciousness see your symbol emerging out of the sky like a UFO.
- Before you ask for your healing-symbol picture a desert. When you make your request to your Higher Consciousness see your symbol emerging like a mirage.
- Before you ask for a healing-symbol take a notepad and a pen. When you make your request to your Higher Consciousness let your hand write down an idea of a symbol. Alternatively you can let your hand draw a symbol.
- Before you ask for your healing-symbol imagine a radio. When you make your request to your Higher Consciousness hear a response coming from this radio.
- Before you ask for your healing-symbol take a medium-sized piece of clay or something similar in your hands. When you make your request to your Higher Consciousness let your hands form a rough symbol.
- If a friend or a therapist is guiding you through this part of symbol therapy they can ask your

Higher Consciousness for a healing-symbol for you. They should ask in the following way: 'Higher Consciousness, can you please give (your name) a healing-symbol to overcome his/her suffering from feeling (name the problem) for the highest good of all beings.' You need to listen to their request and pay attention to whatever appears in your mind.

Last but not least thank your Higher Consciousness for its help once you have received your healing-symbol and once you are satisfied with the symbol of your choice.

SUMMARY

• Ask for your healing-symbol in the following way: 'Higher Consciousness (or whatever name you call it), can you please give me a healing-symbol to overcome my suffering from feeling (name the problem) for the highest good of all beings.' The process of symbol therapy will be much more effective when you ask in this open way instead of telling your Higher Consciousness how you want your problem to be solved.

• Always add 'for the highest good of all beings' because this altruistic motivation will bring you into closer contact with your Higher Consciousness.

• You can pick the healing-symbol that feels right for you and you can check with your Higher Consciousness if you feel unsure about your choice. Your healing-symbol should have a beautiful and bright colour.

• If you have difficulties in receiving a healing-symbol refer to the list of remedies above.

–10–
Breathe your
healing-symbol

*B*REATHING THE HEALING-SYMBOL is the part of the practice that will bring about the actual transformation of your problem. Before you start to breathe take a moment or two to wish yourself the best. Tell yourself: '*I always love myself deeply with all my problems and weaknesses and I especially love myself with my suffering from feeling (name your problem).*'

These few moments of loving yourself are essential for symbol therapy to work. Whenever you breathe your symbols, always start with this sentence and a few seconds of wishing yourself well.

Why is loving yourself so important? The core of all happiness is feeling connected to others and to yourself in love and the core of love is to have well-intentioned wishes. Good wishes and love are prerequisites for any positive transformation to take place and at the same time they are part of the improvement itself. Genuine love for yourself will cause you to relax so that a transformation of your problems can happen much more easily. On the other hand – disapproving of yourself or even hating yourself will make you tense and in this rigid state nothing can change. Resentment of yourself or of your particular problem will work as a block to the process of turning unhappiness into happiness. It will create a feeling of being separated and cut off and it is precisely those feelings which are at the core of all unhappiness.

It is easy to love the parts of ourselves which are already perfect. But if we want to solve our problems and transform them we need to widen our love to take in the parts of us which are imperfect. This is why you should say: *'I always love myself deeply with all my problems and weaknesses and I especially love myself with my suffering from feeling (name your problem).'*

Think about a relationship in which you feel you are genuinely loved. Isn't it much easier to adapt to this person and to find compromises with him or her than it is with somebody who is repeatedly critical of you? Change and transformation can happen much more easily in loving surroundings and are blocked by aversion and hatred.

For the transformation in symbol therapy to happen you do not have to be dependent on somebody else to love you. You can simply love yourself. And at the same time this love for yourself is part of the solution to your problem. No matter why you are suffering, more love is always part of the answer. Even if your problem is physical or financial, more love will help you to relax and be more content despite external problems and adversity.

Loving ourselves is something we can easily talk about but for many of us it is awkward to practise. For some people it even feels wrong, as if it will make them more self-indulgent, vain or arrogant. If you feel like this try to make your heartfelt good wishes not only for yourself but for everybody else as well. From a spiritual point of view this is an even more advanced practice.

But generally speaking simply loving ourselves and wishing ourselves well will make us into more confident, loving and happy people who genuinely have something to give to others. There is nothing strange about loving yourself. People who have received an abundance of love throughout their childhood and as adults love themselves as the most natural thing in the world. They are often not even aware of it because for them it's second nature. It's those among us who haven't received an awful lot of love throughout our lives who find it most difficult to love ourselves. But we are the ones who need this love most urgently. If you find it difficult to love yourself here is a little exercise you can use that might help you.

Developing more love for yourself

- Remember a moment in your life when you deeply loved another being. They might have been your baby, your partner or a pet.
- When you feel this love, turn it towards yourself without changing it and without thinking about

it a lot. Feel this love for yourself. Open up to it
and really take it in.

• Start to talk to yourself in the same loving way
that you would talk to someone you love. Speak
about your problems in a compassionate,
soothing way, as you would talk to a helpless
child. The part of yourself which can't solve
your problem yet is like that helpless child. It
needs love and encouragement. Any scolding
would only make matters worse.

• Do this exercise frequently, until it becomes
second nature.

After you have sent yourself a good measure of love,
imagine or sense your healing-symbol in your spiritual
heart. This is a wonderful place and we will find it in the
middle of our chest beneath the breastbone. It is from
here that our deepest fulfilment and happiness comes.
Our spiritual heart is the source of the love and the wisdom we are all searching for and it is the only place
where unhappiness can be transformed into happiness.
Only through our heart will we ever find our deepest fulfilment because it is the doorway to our Higher
Consciousness. There is no other way to connect with
our Higher Consciousness than through an open and
loving heart. And it is through completely opening and
surrendering our heart that we can finally unite with our
Higher Consciousness and discover that it has always
been our true nature.

At the same time, our heart is the place where we
feel most sensitive and vulnerable. It can feel risky and

even foolish to open it completely and to allow ourselves to be so exposed. We may be afraid that we won't be able to protect ourselves properly any more.

But connecting more to our Higher Consciousness means taking the risk of opening our heart and being unprotected. And that is what makes it so difficult. We want the joy and the happiness that comes with an open heart but we fear being vulnerable and exposed.

Every genuine spiritual path will teach you how you can gently open your heart step by step and overcome the fears that go along with this process. You will learn that the vulnerability of an open heart contains a great strength and you will experience that ultimately nobody can harm it. Your spiritual heart in all its beauty and tenderness is actually indestructible.

In symbol therapy we are most interested in the heart's ability to transform unhappiness into happiness. Remember a time when you felt really unhappy so you talked to somebody about it and afterwards you felt better. What exactly made the shift from unhappiness to happiness? Was it how you analysed the problem when you talked about it? Was it the clarity of the advice you got from the other person? Probably not.

When we are unhappy our heart is closed and we feel better when our heart can open again because this is the only way to reconnect to our love which is the core of happiness. This opening of the heart is most likely to happen when somebody listens to us in a sympathetic and non-judgmental way and appreciates us. The other person's sympathy comes directly from their heart and touches the hardened walls of our heart. When we feel this heartfelt sympathy we may not be able to withhold the tears any more. For a moment everything seems even worse but if we can surrender and allow ourselves to be touched in our most vulnerable spot the walls and knots in our heart will melt away and we'll feel better again. The non-judgmental way in which the other person listens to us gives us space and our heart can relax; a deep sigh of relief comes from our chest and we may find new hope. Finally, the person who has listened to us so lovingly says some very appreciative things about us. Our heart opens to this appreciation like a flower to the sun. Our emotional space widens even further and fresh ideas about how to solve our problem may come to us.

Most of us don't have access to such a wonderful supportive listener all the time. In symbol therapy we do what we can ourselves to gently get in touch with our heart and its power to transform unhappiness into happiness. We do this by loving ourselves and by visualising our healing-symbol in the middle of our heart which is the source of love. In this way the trans-formation of our problem will come from the most loving and sacred place within us and we will reduce the risk of blocking the solution to our problem through resentment of ourselves. Even better, when we work on any problem with symbol therapy we open and release the love of our heart more and more and that will bring us the deepest happiness in the long term.

When our heart has opened up and love is flowing freely we will feel wonderful. We will feel deeply happy and our problems will stop bothering us. Doubts, confusion and neurotic symptoms will fade away and our self-esteem will be so strong that we won't even think about it any more. All our relationships will be easy, even those which were difficult before. In other words, an open, loving heart is part of the solution to all our problems.

If you find it hard to believe in what I have just described, think about the last time you fell deeply in love. The bliss and euphoria we experience in the first delicious encounters with a new love comes from the experience of letting go of our defences and opening our heart and its love to our new lover. Feelings of separateness and isolation suddenly disappear and we start to see the whole world through rose-coloured glasses. Isn't it true that our previous problems bother us less and that we can be more generous and tolerant towards difficult people when we are in love? If we could maintain an open heart beyond the honeymoon we would experience bliss and happiness forever. But, unfortunately, we often return all too soon to the bad habit of putting our own well-being above the well-being of our partner and that is when the arguments start.

If we were able to enter our body and experience our spiritual heart directly we would find only space. This space is as wide as the universe and as bright as the sun and it is vibrant with the beautiful energy of love and joy. It is the true nature of our being and the true nature of our Higher Consciousness. This space is pregnant with all possibilities. Anything can arise from it – even the solution to the problem we are struggling with.

Into this space we place our healing-symbol. We don't think of our heart as a small physical organ but as limitless space vibrating with love and joy. It is from here that new ideas, insights and possibilities arise. Our brain will be activated in the process to receive thoughts, but it is through the heart that we connect to the wisdom of our Higher Consciousness. By putting our healing-symbol into our heart we are able to connect more and more with our Higher Consciousness and we gradually learn to receive the answers to all of our problems.

The next step is to breathe out the colour and the positive qualities of your healing-symbol in a very relaxed, natural way and once again – with as much love as possible. Some people feel this love as a warm positive feeling but for symbol therapy to work it is enough just to be well-intentioned. Simply wish healing and happiness for yourself and everybody concerned in your problem when you breathe out the positive qualities of your healing-symbol. The positive qualities of the symbol are transmitted through its colour and its particular vibration. So you breathe the colour of your healing-symbol lovingly from your heart out into your body and then beyond the boundaries of your body and into your entire aura. (Your aura is an egg-shaped energy field that surrounds your body.) The light will go even further and fill the whole world around you. It includes and envelops everything and everyone that is part of your problem. The light touches both you and the world like a loving gift and transforms everything and everyone for the highest good of everybody concerned. If your problem is in your body as in the case of a physical illness you breathe the colour of your healing-symbol mainly to the part of your body that needs healing but still out into the world as well.

Imagine the symbol as a bright yellow sunflower. Most of us probably have a feeling of what a sunflower might symbolise. It can stand for joy in life, abundance and childlike innocence. All these qualities are contained in its yellow colour. So when you breathe out in a loving way you both feel and see the way your body becomes filled with yellow light and the qualities that go with it. You feel how the vibrant yellow light radiates beyond your body's boundaries, into your aura and out into the world and to its people. In this way your whole being and your whole world becomes filled with your love and the meaning and quality of your healing-symbol.

You don't need to know exactly what qualities your healing-symbol carries. It is enough to have a vague feeling about it. It can be interesting to speculate about the meaning of your healing-symbol but your interpretation is not necessary to the process. It is enough simply to be sure that your healing-symbol does have meaning.

When you have a pink healing-symbol you lovingly breathe out pink light and when you have a blue symbol you breathe out blue light. If you have received a healing-symbol with two or more colours you might find it difficult to visualise and breathe all these colours at once. In that case you can ask your Higher Consciousness to show you which of the colours is the most important. Then you work mainly with this colour.

You breathe the colour and the positive qualities of your symbol into your body and into the world for one relaxed outbreath. Don't strain yourself in any way. It is important to keep your mind and body relaxed and to enjoy the process. The inbreath comes in its own rhythm and while you breathe in you just enjoy the presence of your symbol in your heart. Then you breathe the good qualities of your symbol and its colour out again.

Giving something positive to ourselves and to other people is not what we typically do when we have a problem. Giving often seems the last thing on our mind when we are in pain. What people typically do when they have a problem is look at the world and either blame it for their problem or demand compensation and help. Many people blame themselves as well.

When we breathe out the good qualities of our healing-symbol we do none of this. Although we have a problem, although we are suffering, we focus on giving out lovingly to ourselves and to the world the qualities we have received from our Higher Consciousness. It is this very process of giving which makes us aware that there is an inexhaustible source of joy, love and strength within us. If we try to hold on to the good things we have received from our Higher Consciousness and keep them just for ourselves we lose touch with this source. We have to pass on these wonderful qualities and it is this giving that strengthens our trust that we will never lose this source of love and wisdom. The more we give, the more we are able to take from our Higher Consciousness and this process makes the connection stronger and stronger. In giving out we feel less victimised, less deprived and less helpless – less of all the feelings we have when we blame the world or ourselves for our problems. Instead, we start to feel more confident and strong.

Symbol therapy will help you to find this source of happiness, but don't be disappointed if you don't feel this effect immediately in its full strength. In order to build a strong connection with your Higher Consciousness you need dedication, faith and, most of all, practice. Over time, and if you do symbol therapy regularly, you will find that the effects of the practice become stronger and stronger.

Let me stress again that it is important to do the breathing with as much love as you can. This love is most important to the process of symbol therapy because of its ultimate transformative power. Love is the ideal environment in which we can change and transform with ease. When we feel loved we become soft and flexible so that we can change more easily. But when we feel hated we become rigid and defensive and change is very difficult.

I try to make it a habit always to send love to everything and everybody I find difficult and problematic. I don't do this in order to become a very saintly person but because it works. When I send love to my wounds they heal more quickly. When I send love into my physical pain it often subsides. When I feel upset, sad or angry and I remember to love myself these difficult emotions decrease and my self-confidence rises. And the most amazing results are the ones I get when I can motivate myself to send love to people I find difficult. Suddenly I can see them from another angle and that helps me to understand why these people behave in the way they do. My negative emotional involvement usually stops once I have this understanding and then I often find ways to relate to them in a new and much more satisfactory way.

But sending love to the very thing or person that is causing you all these problems can be quite challenging if you have never done it before. My client Annie was having just this difficulty.

She was struggling with the problem of being over-weight. When I told her that she should breathe the colour and the good qualities of her healing-symbol into the fat of her body with love she looked at me with barely suppressed anger and said: *'I don't love my fat – I hate it!'*

Luckily we were both able to laugh about her anger and I explained to her that breathing with love didn't mean liking her fat and in this way holding on to it. Breathing your healing-symbol with love simply means sending the colour and the positive qualities of your symbol as you would send a loving gift to someone with your best wishes. What counted were her good intentions for her body fat, I told her, and not whether she liked it. However, she had to stop hating her fat.

Annie understood what I meant and she breathed the colour of her symbol into her body with the positive intention that her fat cells should transform in the most healthy and happy way.

It worked! Annie lost all the weight she wanted to without any change to her diet or exercise programme.

However, please don't expect that it will work that easily for everybody. If you want to use symbol therapy for a weight problem you need be open to the solution that will work for you. It might well involve making more changes to your diet and exercise programme than Annie had to.

If there is a person who is involved in your problem and you really dislike this person it can be difficult as well to breathe your healing-symbol with love. In this case you can help yourself in the following way. Breathe the coloured light of your healing-symbol out to the other person and see the colour enveloping them. Imagine that the light has loving and well-meaning qualities and that it will transform them into somebody who is happy, loving and most of all really likeable.

Remember, nobody who is genuinely happy will do you any harm. The difficult people are always those who are suffering, even if their suffering is not very obvious to you and if they seem happy on the surface.

Please don't worry about whether your love is strong enough. Any amount, however small, is good because what matters is that you have a positive intention. You would be completely misguided if you directed the colour of your symbol towards other people or towards your physical problems like a weapon. The colour is not there to dominate or control anything or anybody. Don't even breathe in a forceful way. See the light billowing in colourful clouds rather than in straight beams. Let yourself go into your good intention and surrender. 'Do' as little as possible and let the light expand almost of its own accord.

It is important to trust that the positive qualities of your healing-symbol come directly from your Higher Consciousness and to allow them to penetrate every cell of your being and your whole world. Don't do symbol therapy mechanically. Be as aware as you can of how the qualities of your Higher Consciousness float through your being and through your whole world and how they will heal you and remove your problems.

Breathe your healing-symbol for two minutes at a time. You can put your hands on your tummy to support this process. When you breathe in your tummy moves slightly outwards and when you breathe out it falls back again.

Why do we have to use our breath in the process? Deep breathing has a multitude of beneficial effects on body and mind and I recommend that you study the relevant books on this topic if you are interested. For symbol therapy two effects are most important.

First of all deep breathing invariably makes you feel better. It relaxes your body and mind, it replenishes your energy and it makes you feel more alive. In other words, deep breathing gets your energy moving while calming your mind at the same time. This is very helpful because the transformative processes brought about by symbol therapy can happen more easily when you feel more alive and energetic and when you have a calm mind. If deep breathing is so beneficial, you might ask, why don't we do it all the time?

Well, there are some 'disadvantages' to deep breathing. It gets us to participate more fully in life and to feel more feelings. This might sound like a great idea but in reality most of us don't like it. We prefer to stay safely within our familiar limitations and feeling more feelings can even seem scary. But you don't need to worry about this. Symbol therapy will take care of these 'fears'. It is a thoroughly positive approach to problems and you don't need to be afraid that any upsetting feelings or memories which you can't deal with will come up in the process.

The second benefit of conscious deep breathing is that it is an excellent tool for focusing attention in meditation. For our purposes here, breathing helps you to concentrate on the practice of symbol therapy. You might be surprised how difficult it is to focus on your healing-symbol even for two minutes. When you connect your practice to your breathing you will find this becomes much easier.

Sometimes people have problems when they try breathing exercises. They suddenly become short of breath or breathe in a strained and unnatural way. If this happens to you forget about the breathing. Just drop it completely. Focus on your healing-symbol and send its good qualities out without connecting the process to your breath. If that works for you it is better than creating new problems with the breathing part of the practice.

SUMMARY

• Before you start breathing your healing-symbol tell yourself: 'I always love myself deeply with all my problems and weaknesses and I especially love myself with my suffering from feeling (name the problem).'

• When you visualise your healing-symbol in your spiritual heart you will connect more with the heart's ability to transform unhappiness into happiness. An open and loving heart is part of the solution to all of your problems.

• Exhale the colour of your healing-symbol into your body, into your aura and into the world that surrounds you. Do this in a relaxed way and with as much love as possible and include everything and everyone that is involved in your problem. When you breathe in just enjoy the presence of your healing-symbol in your heart. Breathe like this for two minutes at a time.

• Giving something positive out will make you more aware and help you to connect with an inexhaustible source of joy, love and strength inside yourself.

−11−
Ask for your problem-symbol

*A*T *THIS* *POINT* *YOU* need to ask your Higher Consciousness for a symbol that will show you the current state of your problem. This symbol is called the problem-symbol. It will give you feedback from your Higher Consciousness on the progress you are making in your self-development.

Let me give you an example. When I first moved to England I felt pretty homesick for at least a year. At some point I realised that this homesickness wouldn't go away of its own accord and I asked for a healing-symbol to overcome the suffering from it. I got the image of a woman with outstretched arms. Then I asked my Higher Consciousness for a symbol that would show me the current state of my suffering from homesickness, the problem-symbol. I got the image of a woman crouching down hugging herself tightly. It was quite a dramatic picture but it made sense. It showed me that I wasn't open to my new environment and that I was trying desperately to protect myself.

I practised my healing-symbol for one week and although I felt less homesick I still didn't feel really good. To check my progress I asked my Higher Consciousness to show me through my problem-symbol where I was with my problem at the present moment. I got a picture of a woman who was still hugging herself, but she wasn't crouching any more. She was half standing. This picture encouraged me because I realised that all I 'had to do' was to really stand up and stretch out my arms and I knew I was on the right track.

After another week my problem-symbol showed me a woman who was standing straight with her arms slightly apart. I was very satisfied with this result and I knew that it was only a small step to being completely free of my homesickness. By this point I really felt much better about being in England and my deep-seated resistance to my new environment had nearly gone.

From that point onwards I practised my healing-symbol to overcome my suffering from homesickness only on the occasions when I actually felt homesick again, which was less and less often.

After another month I asked for my problem-symbol again and, sure enough, it showed a woman with outstretched arms. My healing-symbol and my problem-symbol had become one.

In fact I had already started to tell everybody that I liked England even more than my home country. So in a way I knew that my symbols had merged even before I checked them. My positive feeling has stayed with me ever since. Thanks to my Higher Consciousness my suffering from homesickness had been overcome once and for all.

Your problem-symbol will give you feedback about the extent to which you have overcome your suffering from your problem. In this respect it is similar to the feedback that you get from measuring your suffering on the scale of zero to ten. The difference is that your problem-symbol is feedback directly from your Higher Consciousness. When you measure your suffering on the scale you give feedback to yourself from your personal consciousness. Both forms of feedback are important and valuable. They give you evidence that symbol therapy is really working for you.

When you ask for your problem-symbol you should do it in the following way:

'Higher Consciousness, can you please give me a symbol that shows my current state of suffering from feeling . . . '
(name what you are suffering from as specifically as you can)

Sometimes you will get a problem-symbol that is somehow connected to your healing-symbol as in my example above. But sometimes you might get very different symbols, which don't seem to have anything to do with each other. Here are some examples of symbols which people have received in their work with symbol therapy.

Suffering	Healing-symbol	Problem-symbol
• Worries about money	A sack with gold-coins	A person in a prison
• Feeling easily hurt by criticism	A blue star	A black star
• Problems in a relationship	A red rose	The rose is withering
• Physical pain	A blue stream	A blue stream with a black stripe in it

Sometimes you can receive problem-symbols which seem quite catastrophic and you might wonder if your problem is really that bad. But you don't need to worry about this. When your problem improves your problem-symbol will improve as well.

My client, Robert, ran his own business and he had a problem with keeping agreements. He had caused countless frustrations to himself and to his employees by constantly forgetting what he had promised and by never being on time. Despite his best intentions he found it hard to change his bad habits. When he asked his Higher Consciousness for a healing-symbol he received a golden bell. His problem-symbol was shown to him as a darkened sky as it is shortly before a thunderstorm. Robert found this problem-symbol a bit startling and he didn't like it very much.

When we met two weeks later he told me that he had definitely improved in keeping his agreements. However, there had still been a few occasions when he had been late. He had measured his suffering on the scale at five when we had first met and now his suffering was down to three.

Then Robert relaxed deeply and asked his Higher Consciousness to give him a symbol that would show him the current state of his suffering from feeling frustrated from not keeping agreements. Instead of the initial dark sky he got a picture that showed lots of little grey clouds in a blue sky. The thick grey clouds from before had dissolved, but there were still grey clouds in the sky. Robert was relieved to get a 'better' problem-symbol and told me that his new problem-symbol mirrored exactly how he felt. After another two weeks he asked for his problem-symbol again. This time he got an image of even smaller grey clouds. His suffering on the scale was down to two-and-a-half.

After this, Robert's old negative patterns returned from time to time. But after another two months, and with the help of a management-seminar he attended, his problem seemed to be completely resolved. He changed a lot of the procedures in his business and learnt a new and much more effective way of keeping a diary. His suffering on the scale was down to 0.25 and when he asked for his problem-symbol again he got his initial healing-symbol – a golden bell in a blue sky!

As with the healing-symbol you don't need to accept every problem-symbol that is shown to you. You can ask for another one if you have some reason for not liking the one you are shown. But obviously the problem-symbol is more negative and less attractive than the healing-symbol anyway. This will change over the course of the following few weeks as the problem-symbol will become more and more beautiful. After you have received your problem-symbol thank your Higher Consciousness again for its help.

SUMMARY

• Get feedback on your process by asking your Higher Consciousness for your problem-symbol in the following way: 'Higher Consciousness, can you please give me a symbol that shows my current state of suffering from feeling (name the problem).'

• Pick the symbol that feels right to you.

• As your problem improves your problem-symbol will change into something more beautiful according to the progress you are making. The way your problem-symbol changes can give you guidance about how to solve your problem.

–12–
Work with your healing-symbol for two weeks

N*OW YOU HAVE FINISHED* the part of symbol therapy that you do in deep relaxation and the 'real work' begins. In order to get lasting results with symbol therapy you have to work with your healing-symbol for a two-week period. It consists of two minutes twice a day during which you need to visualise and breathe the colour and the good qualities of your healing-symbol as described earlier. Start your two-minute symbol therapy session by telling yourself that you always love yourself deeply with all your problems and weaknesses, and that you love yourself especially with your suffering from feeling the way you do.

Most people will agree that it is always possible to squeeze four minutes into their daily routine no matter how tight their schedule. So not having enough time can't be a real hindrance if the practice takes only four minutes a day. The real difficulty seems to be getting into the habit of doing the practice.

The easiest way of creating a new habit is to combine it with a habit you already have. One way of doing this is to do two minutes of symbol therapy first thing in the morning and last thing at night. Another way is to always do it after you have cleaned your teeth. One of my clients always does it on the train to and from work. If you already have a prayer or meditation routine you are a step ahead of many people as you can easily include symbol therapy in your existing ritual.

It usually won't work if you just 'try to remember' to do the symbols. After an enthusiastic start most people who try this find that more often than not they forget to do their short practice. After this has happened often enough they give up. It is sad when a method as effective as symbol therapy fails because it simply gets forgotten.

It is a good idea to create some ways of helping yourself to remember your practice. You can put slips of paper with a reminder around the house, or you can make notes in your diary, or you can add it to the list of things you do each day.

When you do your practice it is best to try to find a time when you have enough peace and quiet to fully concentrate on it. But don't worry if you can't focus fully on your symbol therapy because you are trying to do it while you are chatting to your colleague during a lunch-break. It is certainly better to do it in that situation than not at all.

Some people complain that they fall asleep if they do symbol therapy while lying in bed. There is a simple remedy for this problem. You just need to prop yourself up in bed in a sitting position while you do the practice. After just two minutes you can drop down and rest peacefully!

What should you do when you forget to do your symbol therapy practice? You need to work with your healing-symbol twice a day for two weeks which makes twenty-eight times. If you forget for a day or two you can simply add them on at the end of your two weeks. If on average you forget half of your sessions then visualise and breathe your symbol for four weeks instead of two. Don't be put off if you frequently forget your exercise. It doesn't matter how often you forget it. All that matters is that you don't give up altogether. So you can always start again even if you have forgotten to do your practice for a very long time.

Human beings are creatures of habit and are generally slow to change. If we want to change we need a certain amount of repetition. As a minimum, two weeks of doing symbol therapy twice a day or twenty-eight times altogether have brought good results.

If you do less than this you might get good results but they may not last. Sometimes people work with a symbol for a few days and as soon as their problem improves they stop. This is not advisable because often the problem will quickly return. When you do just a few repetitions the transformation is often not deep enough.

In addition to this, you can breathe your symbol when your problem becomes acute. You don't need to interrupt your activity to do this. It is enough if your symbol flickers through your mind every now and then and if you think vaguely of the colour radiating through your body and beyond. You can do this while you are having a conversation, while you are reading or while you are working. Just make sure that you stay relaxed and that you not starting to 'fight' your problem. Don't try to improve the process of symbol therapy by straining. Making too much effort will not work – on the contrary, the more relaxed you are when you use this method the better results you will have because your Higher Consciousness will have more space in which to unfold its good qualities.

Barbara had problems with feeling depressed. As recommended she visualised her symbol twice a day, as well as when she felt her depression coming on. To her amazement she found that the mere thought of her symbol reduced the severity of her usual depression by half. After working with some other symbols and making some changes in her life her depression disappeared altogether.

If, for example, you are doing symbol therapy for being overweight you can think of your healing-symbol every time you want to eat and while you are eating. Be open to the changes that this might create in your eating habits.

You need to wish with all your heart for your problem to be removed but you mustn't have preconceptions about how this improvement should come about. Be open to solutions you would never have thought of before. The solution might be even the exact opposite of what you thought should happen. Do whatever you can to improve your situation but don't try to control every detail of the process. Your Higher Consciousness is trying to help you, so leave some space for this help to manifest.

It might happen that because you are using symbol therapy your problem is more on your mind than usual. This can actually be helpful because in this way you can look at it more closely and find solutions more easily. I have never observed that symbol therapy made somebody feel worse or brought up material they couldn't deal with. It is a very efficient method designed to make you happy in the most effective way possible.

But please don't expect miracles after you have done symbol therapy for the first couple of times. Some people have had very fast results but it can also take a bit longer. Sometimes you might feel no change whatsoever for ten days and then you might have a small breakthrough or a big one.

Sometimes people have come back to me and said that their symbol therapy hasn't worked for them. When we have examined what happened it has often turned out that their healing-symbol changed of its own accord or that they have changed it themselves. This is what happened to Mary. She had been working on her problem of loneliness quite successfully. When we first met she had been suffering considerably from having no partner and she had been a seven on the scale of suffering. After four weeks of symbol therapy her suffering was down to a one, although she still hadn't found a partner. She felt much better but really couldn't explain why. However, when she came to our next session she again felt dreadful. When I asked her what had happened she told me that she had felt that her healing-symbol had gradually 'lost its power'. She hadn't felt excited by it any more and she had found it harder and harder to visualise it in its original form (a happy person standing on top of a mountain). The symbol seemed to be changing and was becoming more and more similar to her problem-symbol, which was a lonely woman in the rain. Mary was just going along with this process and was visualising the symbol in its new form. Not surprisingly she was feeling worse and worse.

I explained to Mary that the forces in her that had created her suffering had started to dominate the forces that came from her Higher Consciousness. I could see this because the healing-symbol which her Higher Consciousness had given her had changed into something more similar to her problem-symbol. In practising this new, more negative symbol, she was giving in to her inner negativity. This was why she was feeling much worse again.

What Mary was experiencing was a process which is extremely common and which everybody experiences much of the time. In Christian terminology it is known as the fight between God and the devil. In Buddhist terminology it is known as the process whereby our ego overshadows our true nature. A psychologist would say that our neurotic tendencies have become stronger again.

It really doesn't matter how you describe this process. The only thing that matters is that you stay in your healthy positive side as much as you can. Within the framework of symbol therapy this means that you need to maintain your healing-symbol in exactly the way it was given to you by your Higher Consciousness. *Never allow your healing-symbol to change of its own accord and you must never change it yourself.*

If you find it hard to visualise your healing-symbol in the form that it was given to you, you still need to try to visualise it in its original form as precisely as you can. Every time your symbol seems to change its form or colour, let this image gently go and return to your original healing-symbol. It doesn't matter how often you have to repeat this process because it will not weaken the positive effects of symbol therapy. Just continue with your practice as well as you can.

If for some reason you feel that you really want a new healing-symbol before your two weeks' period is up, you must ask your Higher Consciousness.

The healing-symbol can't really lose its power because it is your faith and concentration that enable your symbol to be charged with the energy of your Higher Consciousness. If it feels as if your symbol has lost its power it is more likely that your concentration and faith are not as strong as they were. Variations in the amount of concentration and faith a person has are absolutely normal. We are never the same, not even for two seconds. The remedy for these natural swings is repetition. Stick to your symbol and visualise it as well as you can and that will be good enough.

Doing symbol therapy does not always feel exciting and intense – it can even feel boring. You do not always get an immediate effect and things don't necessarily change as soon as you start the practice, although this may well happen. Usually symbol therapy is more like taking tablets. You swallow two in the morning and two in the evening and things gradually get better (without side-effects). And you mustn't change your medication without asking your doctor. In this case, of course, the doctor is your Higher Consciousness.

Generally speaking, you can't overdo symbol therapy. Even if you breathe your healing-symbol for several hours a day you will not get any negative side-effects. Still, this amount of practice is neither necessary nor particularly beneficial. On the contrary, if you do practice your symbol for a very long time your inner attitude can easily become a little aggressive, trying to fight and conquer your problem with the beautiful light of your symbol. But this is not how the practice works. Symbol therapy works through love and wisdom and not through aggression, no matter how subtle it is.

The human mind seems to need time and frequent reminders to make lasting changes. However, people sometimes believe that in order to overcome their problems all they need is one amazing breakthrough in which everything becomes clear and their problem is solved once and for all. In reality it doesn't work like this. Many problems are nothing other than habits of negative thinking and negative feelings. In order to overcome them we need to let them go and replace them with healthier thinking and more joyful feelings. This might sound terribly simplistic and unexciting but when it comes to changing the human mind it boils down to just that. Even if you have deep insights and amazing liberating experiences the transformative results of these will be short-lived if you don't have a method to engrain the changes they bring about into your mind. Repeating your symbol twice a day over the course of two weeks is a means of achieving this, even if it seems boring.

Some people try to change their negative habits of thinking and feeling just with their will-power. This usually doesn't work because this approach doesn't take into account the fact that a part of our self unconsciously wants to hold on to our problem. My client Paul was a good example of this. He had problems with commitment in his relationships with women and had just left his wife. He had moved in with his girlfriend but they were arguing a lot because she wanted more commitment than he was willing to give. Paul had spent a lot of his adult life under the influence of drugs and alcohol and had made only a half-hearted commitment to stopping this. He was pretty depressed about his whole situation but he was motivated to bring about some change. His favourite approach was to use affirmations. He used to say positive affirmations to himself and if he felt he was resisting them he simply repeated them to himself as often as possible. But his problems didn't change one iota. He was as depressed as before, he argued with his girlfriend as much as before and he continued to feel guilty about his wife. Why was this?

Paul had deep-seated problems that had been covered up for many years by his addictive behaviour. He was completely unconscious of why he couldn't commit to a relationship, why he continually made the women he was with unhappy or why he was so depressed. The use of positive affirmations such as: '*I am fully alive and happy*' or '*I now commit joyfully*' did not help him. On the contrary they usually made him feel worse. The more he tried to talk himself into these affirmations, the more the impulse not to commit surfaced and the more a voice in his head told him that his life was meaningless. But Paul was undeterred and struggled on repeating his sentences in the hope that one day he would break through his own resistance. But it didn't work.

If you think about it, it couldn't work. Using affirmations in the way Paul did was an act of aggression against himself. He was using them like a weapon against his own negativity. What Paul didn't know was that you can't destroy thoughts or feelings or get rid of them. It is just not possible because they are part of our mind and the mind can't be destroyed. Trying to stop yourself thinking and feeling in a certain way is like trying to stop a stream of water with your hands. No matter how skilfully you place your hands, the water will always find a way around them. And the water will flow with even greater force because the partial damn you've built with your hands creates pressure. This is why Paul felt even worse when he used his affirmations. His negative impulses came through with even stronger force. Another thing that made Paul feel worse was dwelling on his unhappy childhood. Unfortunately he felt strongly compelled to do just that. As he attempted to discover 'the reasons' for his current problems he found more and more sad memories that made him unhappy. When I explained to Paul how he was inflicting suffering on himself by dwelling on his childhood he agreed with me but he found it hard to give this habit up.

Paul is not untypical. For most of us it takes time and self-awareness to realise how fruitless these approaches to resolving our problems are.

Some people believe that it is possible to 'let feelings out' in order to get rid of them and sometimes we indeed feel better after a good cry or after exploding with anger. But people who express emotions *frequently* and *powerfully* will discover that their emotions don't decrease – on the contrary they increase. This is as true for negative emotions as for positive ones. When someone habitually expresses joy they become more joyful and when they habitually express anger and sadness they become more angry and sad.

The reason for this is that the human mind likes to create habits. Habitually expressed emotions are like a stream running down a mountainside. The longer and the more forcefully you express your emotions the more deeply the stream carves out its bed. This stream-bed is the habit we create by expressing our emotions and the longer we do it the more difficult it becomes to change the habit. Habitually letting out emotions makes them stronger, not weaker.

Everybody experiences disturbing thoughts and emotions from time to time and many of us would like to avoid them or get rid of them as quickly as possible. Unfortunately, it is impossible to cut out negative feelings in the same way that you cut out an infected appendix. If we only learn on our path of self-development that it is impossible to erase our negative thoughts and feelings by will-power, we will spare ourselves a lot of unnecessary suffering. This endless fight against our own mind takes up a lot of our time and energy and yet it is completely futile. It is possible to have short-lived successes in fighting certain negative thoughts and feelings but as soon as we are not on guard the negativity comes back, often even more strongly than before. So the obvious question is: *What can we do with negative thoughts and feelings?*

Have you ever tried to cheer up an unhappy toddler? It is very interesting because when it comes to emotions we are not that different from a toddler. Imagine your toddler is crying piteously. If you ignore him he will most likely scream even more loudly to get your attention. It is the same with ourselves. When we feel bad and try to ignore our feeling it will often get stronger and demand our attention. This is the first step: we need to turn our attention towards our feeling and stop ignoring it in the same way we would turn towards our crying toddler. It seems natural to take our unhappy child in our arms, stroke him lovingly and whisper soothing words into his ear. If we talk angrily to him or try to ridicule him for crying he will become even more upset because we are adding insult to injury. In the same way, our own negative feeling will increase if we tell ourselves off for it or ridicule ourselves. Can we do for ourselves what we would naturally do for our child? Can we 'take ourselves into our own arms' and whisper comforting loving words into our own inner ear? We need this in the same way that a toddler needs it and it is the only thing that will work at this point. Often our toddler will calm down and run off to play if we comfort him. But sometimes he just won't stop crying. We then have to discover what we can do to make him feel better. We might have to retrieve the toy another child has taken from him or we might have to put him to bed if he is tired. As adults we have to do the same. If we don't feel better after comforting ourselves we might need to face and resolve conflicts with other people or we might need to make appropriate changes to our lifestyle. But sometimes our toddler still won't stop even when we have done everything we can think of to improve his situation. He whinges and wails and rolls around on the floor in utter misery. On an adult level this is like being stuck in a vicious circle of an ever repeating emotion which has no real cause. We need to be very skilful to resolve this problem whether with our toddler or with ourselves. When we feel our child really hasn't got any more reason to go on whimpering we might gently try to tickle him or to make him laugh in some other way. If we are lucky, it will work and after having some fun with each other he will go off and play. On an adult level at this stage we need to develop some humour about ourselves and our 'terrible' emotions. If we manage to have a loving yet humorous attitude towards ourselves we might master the high art of letting our feelings go without suppressing them. From this space new ideas or a change of perspective can arise and we feel better. So we have three steps to deal with negative emotions:

1 Comfort
2 Resolution
3 Humour

Although these steps can happen almost simultaneously we need to go through them in their proper order. If we try to resolve our problem or to be humorous too early it can have the opposite of the desired result. But if we only give ourselves comfort we might not do what is necessary to resolve our problem. Symbol therapy can greatly support you in this process. It will help you to pacify your emotions and it will give you the necessary insights about what to do in order to avoid future negativity.

When my client Paul used symbols, his situation improved. He did what he had avoided doing all his life and what he feared most of all. He talked openly to his wife and to his girlfriend and started to relate to them in a more honest way. This was a major breakthrough for him because throughout his adult life Paul had never related to anyone in an honest way. His relationships had always been riddled with lies and dishonesty. For him to have the courage to talk to somebody honestly was like experiencing a mini-enlightenment. His depression lifted considerably and by the time that he stopped coming to me he was about to move out of his girlfriend's flat. It had become clear to him that he was at a stage in his life where he didn't want to make a commitment and that it was in the best interest of everybody that he lived on his own for a while. Finding out why he had become a drug addict with all the accompanying dishonesty had been completely irrelevant to his process of improvement.

SUMMARY

• Breathe the colour and the positive qualities of your healing-symbol for two minutes twice a day for two weeks. Always start the two minutes by telling yourself: 'I always love myself deeply with all my problems and weaknesses and I especially love myself with my suffering from feeling (name the problem).'

• Don't worry if you sometimes forget to do your symbol therapy. Just add enough sessions on so that you have done them twenty-eight times.

• You can breathe your healing-symbol in any situation in which your problem becomes acute. Do this in as relaxed and loving a way as possible.

• Always visualise your healing-symbol in exactly the same form and colour as it was shown to you by your Higher Consciousness. Never allow your healing-symbol to change of its own accord and you must never change it yourself.

• Work with your healing-symbol for two weeks. Don't stop sooner if your problem improves before the end of this period or if you haven't had amazing results after a few days.

−13−
Get feedback on your progress

*A*FTER THE FIRST TWO WEEKS OF symbol therapy are finished there are two ways in which you can check on your progress. The first method is to ask yourself where you are on the scale of suffering. You can do this either every fortnight or once a week. If you ask yourself this question every day it can become confusing because your numbers on the scale can fluctuate quite a bit. It is best if you ask yourself where you are on the scale of suffering, taking an average of the last three days. Then compare this number with the number you got when you first asked this question.

It often happens that people have quite dramatic improvements. They might measure their suffering the first time as a seven or an eight and after two weeks they might be down to a two or a three. But even if you don't get this major improvement your number should have gone down at least two points after the first two weeks of symbol therapy. That is the minimum improvement you can expect.

If you feel that your suffering has gone down only one point on the scale something has gone wrong. Maybe you didn't define your problem in the proper way or maybe you didn't ask for your healing-symbol in the prescribed form. Maybe you didn't like your healing-symbol or it didn't have a beautiful bright colour. Perhaps you have changed your healing-symbol or you might even have forgotten to ask your Higher Consciousness for it. And if you have resisted putting your ideas about how to change your situation into practice, symbol therapy will not bring good results either. You can check where you might have gone wrong in the previous chapter about trouble-shooting.

However, no matter how small your improvement, the important thing is that you carry on with symbol therapy. If you persevere you are bound to get good results in reducing your suffering from anything that troubles you.

The second way to get feedback about your progress is to ask your Higher Consciousness to show you your problem-symbol. This is a more intuitive approach, compared with the scale-question which is a more rational way of getting feedback. It is always good to use both methods so you use all your abilities – reason and intuition.

Before you ask for your current problem-symbol recall the problem-symbol that was given to you in the beginning. If you have made progress with your problem you will now be shown a new problem-symbol that is not as negative as the previous one. In order to ask for your problem-symbol you need to relax as much as you can again. Then you can ask your Higher Consciousness as before:

> *Higher Consciousness, can you please give me a problem-symbol that shows my current state of suffering from feeling . . .'*
> *(name what you are suffering from as specifically as you can)*

When you ask for your problem-symbol and you are shown a beautiful symbol, or even your healing-symbol, you have reached your aim and your problem is solved.

Sometimes people find it a bit difficult to interpret the changes in their problem-symbol and wonder whether it is really showing any positive development. *'My problem-symbol has disintegrated into small pieces'*, they might say and ask, *'Is this a positive or a negative development?'*. Actually this does indicate an improvement because it shows that their 'big and solid' problem is starting to break down into more manageable pieces. When I ask my clients if my interpretation is in alignment with how they actually feel they always agree. Symbols seem to have a fascinating ability to exactly mirror the complex life-situation of a person.

Usually you don't need any interpretative skills to evaluate whether your problem-symbol has changed for the better. In most cases it is totally obvious. However, to remove any doubts you might have, the following list tells you how to recognise whether your problem-symbol has improved. Signs that your changing problem-symbol indicates an improvement include:

- The colour of the problem-symbol becomes more beautiful, brighter, lighter or shinier.
- The material the problem-symbol is made of becomes more precious.
- The problem-symbol disintegrates into smaller pieces.
- The problem-symbol becomes more pleasant and attractive.
- Negative aspects of the problem-symbol diminish.
- New positive aspects of the problem-symbol appear.

Here are some examples of how my clients' and my own problem-symbols have changed:

Problem-symbol at the beginning of symbol therapy	Problem-symbol after doing symbol therapy for a while	Problem-symbol after problem has been solved
• Big rock	Many small pebbles	Beautiful sandy beach
• Vicious dragon	Dragon fast asleep	Beautiful cuddly kitten
• Big bush with lots of thorns	Two twigs with thorns	Beautiful palace appears behind the thorns
• Big lump of dark dirty wood	The wood is lighter and shiny	The wood has turned into gold

Some people go through a lot more steps in their changing problem-symbol and the way it changes can give
them clues about the direction in which they need to go
in order to solve their problem. In this way your changing problem-symbol can also help you by giving you
guidance. Do you remember my problem with homesickness, described in Chapter 11? My problem-symbol
was a woman crouching down and it showed me that I
had to stop protecting myself so desperately. Instead, I
had to take the risk of opening up to my new environment. Of course, this seems a quite obvious solution
when you look at the problem from the outside. But
when we are suffering we are often confused about where
and how to find a solution. I have seen many cases in
which a changing problem-symbol provided guidance
for people and helped them turn away from the road that
was leading to more suffering and pursue a way that led
to more happiness instead.

Gary, for example, suffered from feeling exhausted
and tired. When he asked for a problem-symbol he saw
himself in a prison. He found this problem-symbol a bit
shocking at first but then with a sigh of relief he
admitted that he sometimes really felt he was in a prison.
After two weeks of working with his healing-symbol
Gary asked to be shown his problem-symbol again. He
still saw himself in the prison but now there was a door.
This coincided with his plan to take more time to
meditate and to see an acupuncturist. Gary always had a
tendency to think that he wasn't doing enough for his
family and so it wasn't easy for him to take more time for
himself. But he trusted that his Higher Consciousness

was helping him find a solution that was best for his whole family. The positive development in his problem-symbol gave him reassurance that he was on the right track. After two more weeks Gary's problem-symbol showed him opening the door of his prison. He was now regularly taking time to meditate and he felt much less tired although he hadn't started his acupuncture yet. After yet more time and with the help of his acupuncturist the problem-symbol showed him walking through the door towards a brilliant sun, which was his healing-symbol.

SUMMARY

• After two weeks measure your suffering again on the scale and compare the number with the one you had two weeks earlier. You can expect to be at least two points lower on the scale.

• Ask your Higher Consciousness for your current problem-symbol and compare it with the one you received two weeks earlier. Ask in the following way: 'Higher Consciousness, can you please give me a problem-symbol that shows my current state of suffering from feeling (name the problem).'

• Your problem-symbol will improve and change into a more beautiful and pleasant symbol according to the progress you have made with your problem.

–14–
Work through complex problems

*I*F YOUR PROBLEM ISN'T completely resolved after two weeks (it probably won't be if it has been a long-standing problem) you can ask for another healing-symbol. It is a good idea to ask now for a healing-symbol for a different aspect of your issue because in that way you can tackle it from another angle or you can address a deeper layer of it.

You don't need a new problem-symbol – you just continue to use the one received when you asked for it the first time. By now it should already have changed a bit. Even if you are working for several two-week periods on different aspects and on different layers of your initial problem, always use the same problem-symbol. It can be fascinating to see how it improves over time. When your problem-symbol has transformed into something beautiful your problem is solved.

When you want to address a complex problem and you know in advance that it has several aspects and layers (like the suffering from a divorce, for example) you need to ask first for a healing-symbol for the whole problem such as 'my suffering from feeling upset about my divorce'. After you have worked for two weeks with this more general definition you need to decide which aspect of the problem is causing you the biggest suffering now. In the case of a divorce, that might be anger, anxiety about loneliness or grief, for example. Ask for a healing-symbol for this new aspect and in this way you work through all the aspects and layers of your problem. The story of Anne will illustrate how to do this.

Anne worked with symbol therapy to recover from the devastating results of her recent divorce. When she came to see me she was in emotional turmoil. Anne's husband had left her to be with another woman and that had come as a complete shock to Anne. She felt anger, grief, longing, sadness, loneliness and she was suffering from insomnia. In our first session Anne asked generally for a healing-symbol to overcome her suffering from feeling devastated by her divorce. She received a golden brooch as her healing-symbol and as her problem-symbol she received a dead tree. Anne cried a lot during her first two weeks of symbol therapy but she felt a genuine process of letting go. She still had waves of despair but when she remembered her healing-symbol she got over these difficult emotions more quickly than before. After two weeks Anne felt a bit better but she was still very unhappy. When she looked at her problem-symbol, the dead tree, it showed a single green leaf. It wasn't a great improvement but this one green leaf was a big encouragement to Anne. I asked her what was causing her the biggest suffering now out of all her remaining symptoms. She said that although she was more able to let her husband go she felt terrified at the prospect of living on her own.

So this time she asked for a healing-symbol to overcome her suffering from feeling frightened of living on her own. She worked painstakingly with her new symbol for another two weeks and her fear diminished considerably. She also started to meet up with a relative and this was a great comfort to her. When she looked at her problem-symbol two weeks later it had several little buds in addition to its first leaf. This was still not a huge improvement but it served Anne again as an encouragement. Once again I asked Anne to find out which of her remaining symptoms was causing her the biggest suffering. After thinking for a while she said that her unfulfilled longing for a new partner was now the worst for her. After two weeks her problem-symbol (the dead tree) showed even more buds and sprouting leaves and once more she selected the aspect of her problem that was causing her the biggest suffering. Now she asked for a symbol to overcome her suffering from being incredibly angry.

At the end of eight weeks of symbol therapy Anne felt much better. Her suffering from her divorce had been an eight on the scale when she had first come to see me, but at the end of the eight weeks she was down to a two on average. Her problem-symbol showed several full grown leaves and many buds. Her emotional state still fluctuated sometimes but all in all she was over the worst.

Just as Anne did, you should first ask for a healing-symbol for the 'whole' problem. Later you need to ask for healing-symbols for each of the aspects of your problem that are causing you the biggest suffering in turn. It is not necessary to analyse your problem a great deal in order to find its most important aspect. Just work with the part of your problem that is causing you the biggest suffering in a very obvious way.

Caroline was working on her problem of low self-confidence. At first she asked for a healing-symbol to overcome her suffering from feeling shy and awkward and had good results with it. Her suffering went down from a five to a three on the scale. Caroline was encouraged by this result but she wanted to get even better. When she was ready to ask for a new healing-symbol she found it difficult to find another angle to her problem. Finally, she decided to ask for a symbol to overcome her suffering from being afraid of other people in social situations. This new healing-symbol worked very well and brought her suffering down to nearly zero.

Sometimes people feel they can't narrow their problem down any further or that they can't find another angle to it and that their current healing-symbol is working in an excellent way. In that case you can use the same healing-symbol for longer than two weeks. You can also use the same healing-symbol for longer than two weeks if you have a relapse with a problem you've worked on before. You just need to remember your previous healing-symbol and use it until the relapse is over. However, sometimes you will need a new healing-symbol for this particular problem and you will have to work for another two-week period on another aspect of your problem to resolve it completely.

Every time you work with symbol therapy you will get insights about yourself and about what is needed to solve your problem. It is important to take these insights seriously, to write them down in a notebook and to follow them up as well as you can.

Anne, for example, realised that she had neglected the fostering of close friendships while she was married, and so, when her husband left her, she found herself completely alone. When Anne did her symbol therapy she saw very clearly that she had to find a friend to talk to. It was not easy for Anne but she finally found the courage to contact a relative and was received with open arms.

SUMMARY

• When your problem hasn't been solved completely after the first two-week period you need to ask for a new healing-symbol in order to address a different aspect or a deeper layer of your problem.

• When you are working with a complex problem start by asking for a healing-symbol for the 'whole' problem. After you have finished your first two-week period of symbol therapy you can work on the different aspects and layers of your problem.

• Don't ask for a new problem-symbol while you are working on the different layers of the same problem. Go on using the one you received when you asked for it the first time. Observe how it changes as you work through the different aspects of your problem.

• You can use the same healing-symbol for longer than two weeks if it works well for you or if you have a relapse with your problem.

—15—
Maximise your results

*A*FTER I HAD BEEN working for quite a while with
symbol therapy I noticed that many of my clients'
and my own problems seemed to disappear readily and
completely but that some problems didn't get much
better than about a one on the scale of suffering. It was
mostly the long-standing and severe problems that were
not easily removed completely. This seemed understandable and somehow acceptable. If someone has been
suffering severely from a problem for many years a one
on the scale of suffering seems like a piece of cake. It can
even seem greedy to want more. However, I wanted
more and at some point I discovered how to get it.

When you are only a one or at most a two on the
scale of suffering you can start to work on maximising
positive beliefs rather than on reducing suffering. To do
this you need at first to formulate a positive statement
about what you want. If your problem is being

unemployed a positive statement could be: '*I have a wonderful job where I can use all my talents.*' If your problem is depression you could state: '*I am full of joy and optimism.*'

These statements need to be in the present tense and fully positive. You mustn't use words such as 'no', 'never' or 'not' etc. Don't even use 'I am free of . . .'.

Once you have found the statement that best describes what you really want you need to picture what you desire as vividly as you can for a minute or two.

In the next step you need to rate on a scale how much you believe that your statement and your images will come true. This is the 'scale of belief'. A zero means that you don't believe that your statement will possibly come true, a five means that you half believe in it and a ten means that you fully believe that your statement will come true.

A good way to find out how much you believe your statement and your images is to check your feelings. The more you believe in your statements and images the more happiness and positive excitement you will feel. The interesting thing is that when you score yourself high on the scale of belief you feel good even when your statement hasn't yet come true. If you fully believe that you will get the job of your dreams you feel wonderful and you are then able to really enjoy the time that you are unemployed. You will not waste your energy and joy by worrying the whole time about whether you will ever find a job again. Fully believing that you will get what you want will give you *instantaneous and genuine* joy and fulfilment.

Margaret was suffering from loneliness and despair because she felt that she would never find a partner. Through doing symbol therapy her suffering had reduced from an eight to one-and-a-half. When she first came to see me she had found her situation as a single person unbearable and now she was quite happy – mostly. She still felt some fear that she might not find a partner ever again because she was already sixty years of age.

I asked her to formulate a positive statement about what she really wanted. At first she said that she wanted to be happy as a single person, but we both knew that this wasn't her most important wish. What she really wanted was a partner. So she formulated the following positive statement: *'I am living in a wonderful relationship.'* Then she tried to picture this for a short while. When I asked her to rate how much she believed that her statement and her image will come true on the scale of belief she answered quickly and with gusto, *'zero!'*.

But, unfortunately, if you can't believe that you can get what you want, this disbelief will work like a barrier. Your negative beliefs will be a real obstacle to attracting and achieving your aim. But if you fully believe that you will get what you are wishing for, it will make you feel good and it will also greatly support the process of you realising your aim.

So, your aim is to be an eight, nine or ten on the scale of belief that your positive statement and images will come true. To achieve this you can use symbol therapy in the following way. You need to ask your Higher Consciousness:

> *'Higher Consciousness, can you please give me a symbol to overcome the suffering that comes from my not fully believing that . . . '*
> *(state here your positive statement as specifically as you can for the highest good af all beings)*

Margaret asked for a healing-symbol to overcome her suffering from not fully believing that she will live in a wonderful relationship. She received a healing-symbol of a golden couple embracing each other. She carried on using the same problem-symbol she had used through-out her process of working with her problem of being single. When she first started she had seen her problem-symbol as a lonely person standing in the middle of a dense forest. As her suffering improved her problem-symbol had changed and she saw the person walking on a wide track in the forest in a fairly good mood.

You must work with the healing-symbol to over-come your suffering from not believing that your positive statement and images will come true in exactly the same way as you worked with your other symbols. You start by telling yourself :

> *'I always love myself deeply with all my problems and weaknesses and even if I continue not to believe that my positive statement and images will come true.'*

Saying this will help you to prevent you resenting yourself for not being able to believe in your positive statement. Any such resentment would only hinder your progress.

Then you need to visualise your new healing-symbol in the middle of your heart as usual and breathe its good qualities and its colour into your body, aura and environment. Do this for two weeks twice a day for two minutes and then you can ask yourself where you are on the scale of belief. You can also ask yourself where you are on the scale of suffering from your original problem. Don't be surprised if your suffering is finally a zero! To make sure you are not fooling yourself ask your Higher Consciousness to show you your problem-symbol.

Margaret breathed her healing-symbol to overcome her suffering from not believing that she could have a wonderful relationship for two weeks and she rose on the scale of belief from a zero to an eight! For the first time she really believed that at the age of sixty she would find a loving partner.

She went down on the scale of suffering from one-and-a-half to a zero. Her Higher Consciousness showed her problem-symbol as a person who had finally left the forest behind and was standing in a wonderful landscape in brilliant and warm sunshine. In other words, Margaret felt really good despite the fact that she still hadn't found her soul mate. When I last spoke to her she still felt fine and she told me about an exciting and promising encounter she had had with a man.

At this point I need to give you a little warning. Working with a healing-symbol to overcome your suffering from *feeling a problem does not have side-effects*, but working with a healing symbol to overcome your suffering from *not believing in your positive aim can have side-effects*. It can actually bring up all the negative beliefs you have about how you will never realise your aim. If this happens you will start to suffer more, not less. But, fortunately, there is an easy solution to this problem. If you feel that working on your beliefs is making you feel worse rather than better, you should at once return to your initial healing-symbol for your problem. You will need to work with it for a little longer and then after a time you can try to work on your negative beliefs again.

SUMMARY

• Once you score only a one or a two on the scale of suffering you can work on maximising positive beliefs rather than on reducing suffering.

• Find out what you really want to happen in your problem area and formulate a positive statement in the present tense. Picture this statement as a reality as well.

• Rate on the scale of belief how much you believe that your statement and images will come true. Zero means that you don't believe it at all and ten means that you fully believe it.

• Ask your Higher Consciousness: 'Higher Consciousness, can you please give me a symbol to overcome the suffering that comes from my not fully believing that ... ' (state here your positive statement for the highest good of all beings).

• Work with your healing-symbol in the usual way by

visualising it in the middle of your heart and breathing its good qualities and its colour into your body, aura and environment. Start by telling yourself: 'I always love myself deeply with all my problems and weaknesses and even if I continue not to believe that my positive statement and images will come true.'

• Use the same problem-symbol that you used before when you were working on this problem and observe how it develops.

• After two weeks rate yourself on the scale of belief and on the scale of suffering. Then ask to be shown your current problem-symbol again.

• If working on your negative beliefs is making you feel worse, go back to your initial healing-symbol and work with it for a while. Then try again.

−16−
Work with several healing-symbols in parallel

MANY PEOPLE FIND THAT once they've started to have successes with symbol therapy they want to use this method to improve more and more aspects of their life. Anne, for example, found that she wanted to work with symbol therapy on her lack of confidence, her frustration about not finding a new partner, her frustration about being overweight and on problems with her job.

At some point many people come to the conclusion that part of their problem is lack of confidence. This is actually a lack of love for themselves and it lies at the root of many problems. It can be helped effectively with symbol therapy.

You can use symbol therapy to work on very small issues as well. For example, a friend of mine was offered a lift to a party. He was pleased with this because it meant that he could have a drink. On the other hand he knew that sitting in the back-seat of a car always made him feel sick. An enthusiastic user of symbol therapy as he was, he at once asked for a healing-symbol to overcome his suffering from feeling sick in the back-seat of cars. He didn't even relax in order to ask for his healing-symbol but just asked for it shortly before he went out. He said it made a huge difference and was very happy with one more success in his 'self-therapy'.

Working on both big and small issues with symbol therapy can be very satisfying and you can ask for as many healing-symbols as you like for any area of your life. Some people become really enthusiastic about the healing-power of symbols and they work with many symbols at the same time. This is a very good idea and you can do it in the following way.

Whenever you find a problem on which you would like to use symbol therapy you can ask for a new healing-symbol with its corresponding problem-symbol at once. Write these symbols down so that you don't forget them. You don't have to work with all these symbols at the same time. In fact, you will often find that many of these problems will improve even though you have hardly thought about their healing-symbols. Sometimes it seems to be enough just to ask for a healing-symbol and to remember it occasionally.

For bigger problems you always need to work with the appropriate healing-symbol for two weeks, but you can visualise and breathe your other healing-symbols as much or as little as you like or need. You should breathe and visualise the different healing-symbols that you want to use – one after the other, for two minutes each.

Then check through your problem-symbols every few weeks in the way I have described. You will find that many little problems will have disappeared completely even if you have hardly spent any time visualising their healing-symbols.

But it is important that you always work on your most urgent problem with your 'priority' healing-symbol for a full two weeks in order to achieve lasting results. If you just practise your healing-symbols at random and you don't make sure you have a priority healing-symbol the results can be disappointing. You might get improvements with your smaller problems but not with your bigger difficulties.

Barbara had recurrent bouts of cystitis and her first request to her Higher Consciousness was for a healing-symbol to overcome her suffering from this illness. When she practised it both her pain and the urge to frequently go to the loo became less. But more importantly she realised that there was a strong connection between the pain in her bladder and her frustration and irritation when things didn't go the way she wished. Although she had worked for just one week with her first healing-symbol she immediately asked for a new healing-symbol to overcome her suffering from frustration and irritation.

From now on she practised two symbols which took eight minutes a day instead of four. Her cystitis got much better but her frequent irritation was a hard nut to crack. Barbara had been an angry person as long as she could remember and it was not easy for her to let go of this deep-seated habit. She needed several two-week periods with different symbols for different aspects of her anger in order to gain more equanimity.

Like Barbara, many people have insights into what their problem is 'really about' when they practise their healing-symbols. When this happens it is best to ask immediately for new healing-symbols for these new aspects of your problem. You can work with these new healing-symbols in parallel to your priority healing-symbol or later on you can make one of them into your new priority healing-symbol and work with it for a complete two-week period.

Old problems on which you have already worked for two weeks can sometimes flicker into life again. This is normal and you just need to remember their old healing-symbol and practise it for a few days until the problem has disappeared again. You can do this in parallel with the other symbols which you are practising at the moment. But if the old problem comes up strongly again you might choose to ask for a new healing-symbol for it and practise it for another full two-week period once you've finished your current symbol.

SUMMARY

• You can work with as many healing-symbols at the same time as you like. Always practise each symbol one after the other for two minutes each.

• Make the healing-symbol for your most urgent problem into your priority symbol and practise it for a whole two-week period. Work with your other symbols in parallel as much or as little as you like. In this way many smaller problems will disappear almost of their own accord while you put most of your energy into your bigger challenges.

−17−
Maintain well-being in all areas of your life

Standard-symbols

THERE IS A LOT more you can do with symbol therapy to help you live a happy and contented life. Besides our major personal problems we all experience little irritations and niggles as well. For example tiredness, stress or performance-anxiety. We all suffer from problems like these from time to time though for most of us they are not big issues but small and unavoidable by-products of being human. But wouldn't it be nice to be able to do something about your tiredness next time you nearly fall asleep while commuting to work? And wouldn't it be great to have a simple but effective method to help you the next time you feel stressed?

You can ask for healing-symbols for small problems like these and you can use these symbols just at the times that you are experiencing one of these negative states.

These symbols are called standard-symbols and you don't
need to work with them for two weeks, nor do you need
to ask for a problem-symbol. All you need to do is to
remember your standard-symbol and to use it each time
you are suffering from one of the following negative states:

- Tiredness
- Stress
- Physical pain
- Nervousness or mild anxiety
- Small irritations in relationships
- Feeling uninspired and dull

You might find other areas where you can use standard-
symbols. Using these symbols will make life easier but
obviously they won't remove all your problems
completely. Besides being a nuisance, some of these
niggles also have a healthy function. Tiredness, for
example, tells you that you need to rest, and pain tells
you that you might need to see the doctor. You will still
need an injection at the dentist if you have always
needed one because the symbol can't take away all the
pain and indeed it shouldn't. But a symbol will probably
reduce the pain and it will help you to cope with it better.
Your standard-symbol for tiredness will help you to cope
better after a bad night but it won't make you able to
sleep half as much as you did before.

My own standard-symbols are a golden hand for
pain, and a sparkling candle for tiredness. For irritation
in relationships I have been given a symbol of a pink
couple embracing each other. It is really nice to have

these little helps at hand when I need them. It makes the unavoidable ups and downs of life more like plain sailing.

If you have a bigger personal problem in any of these areas it is obviously more appropriate to ask for a specific healing-symbol and corresponding problem-symbol and to work with them for the required two-week period.

Strengthening positive beliefs

There is another interesting variant on symbol therapy you can use to achieve more overall well-being. As described in Chapter 15, 'Maximise your results', you can work on maximising positive beliefs in any area of your life. Start by scanning through all areas of your life – money, health, family, relationships, sexuality, emotional well-being, spiritual development, and so on.

If you have any bigger problems in these areas you obviously need to work in the usual way with symbol therapy. But if you feel pretty good already, but you would still like to create more well-being, you can use this technique to strengthen your positive beliefs.

Choose the area you would like to work on and start by formulating a positive statement. For example, you can say: *'I am healthy and radiantly beautiful'* or *'I am highly successful and happy in my work'* or whatever else you wish for. In the next step you need to picture these statements as vividly as you can.

Then you measure on the scale of belief how much you believe that these statements will come true (a ten is fully believing and a zero is not believing at all). If your belief is lower than an eight or a seven, you can ask for a healing-symbol. Ask in the following way:

> *'Higher Consciousness, can you please give me a healing-symbol to overcome the suffering that comes from my not believing that* (say here your positive statement)*, for the highest good of all beings.'*

Practise this healing-symbol in the usual way for two minutes twice a day for two weeks and enjoy the increase in confidence and happiness that ensues as you believe more and more that your statements will come true. But, obviously, remember that these healing-symbols can't guarantee that you will immediately receive whatever you wish for or that you will never be unhappy or ill again. Life is too complex and ultimately it can't be controlled – not even by all these clever symbols. What these healing-symbols can do for you is to remove the blocks to happiness you have created yourself through your own negative beliefs.

If this practice brings up negative feelings of disbelief it is a sign that you are not yet ready to work in this way. Instead you need to work with a healing-symbol to overcome your suffering from feeling (name the problem) in the usual way.

Clearing and harmonising your chakras

According to Tibetan Buddhism we have 72,000 energy channels in our body and five main energy centres which are called chakras. These chakras are located in your lower abdomen, behind your navel, in your heart, in your throat and behind your forehead. With every thought you think, with every feeling you feel and with every movement you make energy moves through your energy channels and through your chakras. Whatever happens in your mind, emotions and body corresponds to a movement or blockage in your energy system and whatever happens in your energy system has an effect on your physical and psychological well-being. If you have an emotional or physical problem of any kind you will find that you have a disharmony or block in one of your chakras as well. And if you have an imbalance or distortion in your energy system you will experience tensions in your body and disturbing thoughts and emotions.

One way of maintaining your overall well-being is to create harmony in your energy system because it will in turn harmonise your mind, body and emotions. Many people who want to work with their energy system do this with practices such as t'ai chi or yoga. Symbol therapy offers you another way of clearing, balancing and harmonising your main energy centres, the chakras.

If you feel a specific problem around one of your chakras, such as a lump in your throat or tension in your chest, you can ask for a healing-symbol and a corresponding problem-symbol to overcome your suffering from this blockage in the usual way. But here comes something new: healing-symbols to harmonise the chakras are not all visualised in the heart but *in the specific chakra* you are working with. If, for example, you want to work on a block in your throat chakra you visualise your healing-symbol in your throat. You let the light of your healing-symbol expand from your throat and fill your body, your aura and your whole environment. If you are working on the navel-chakra you visualise your healing-symbol in your navel and let the light expand from there. Work with these healing-symbols in the usual way for two minutes, twice a day for two weeks. Be prepared to discover what is 'behind' your energy block. You might remember people and events which you had long forgotten and you might suddenly discover how you yourself create your energy-block through certain attitudes and anxieties. However, you still don't need to worry about coming across traumatic material you can't deal with. It is not in the nature of your Higher Consciousness to create more problems for you than you already have – your Higher Consciousness will simply guide you to the solution to your problem in the fastest way possible. Some people will find that their energy-blocks are cleared away very quickly without any further material or insights coming up.

Katy often suffered from an uncomfortable lump in her throat accompanied by feelings of anxiety and depression. Her healing-symbol was shown to her as a bright golden sun and her problem-symbol was herself in an iron cage. She visualised this golden sun in her throat and expanded its light all through her body and beyond. After practising for a few days she felt the lump in her throat melting and the feelings of anxiety and depression decreasing. She recognised that she had always felt this lump when she feared that she couldn't connect with other people in the way she wanted. She also remembered all the arguments she had had with her father when she was an adolescent. Katy realised that the lump in her throat had appeared when she had stopped arguing with him and had become 'a good girl'. Katy found these insights interesting and carried on practising her healing-symbol. She often found that the mere thought of her healing-symbol was enough to help her when she felt that the lump in her throat was returning. When she asked a few weeks later to be shown her problem-symbol, it showed her outside the iron cage.

If you don't feel a particular problem in any of your chakras you can still use symbol therapy to bring them into optimum harmony. Ask for healing-symbols for each of your chakras and practise them once a week or as often as you feel is appropriate. You don't need to ask for any problem-symbols if you are just practising this basic 'energy-system hygiene'. Most people use the symbol of their Higher Consciousness as the healing-symbol for their heart-chakra. The heart-chakra is the doorway to your Higher Consciousness and therefore it is most important to release any blocks you might have in this area. When your heart is open and your love is flowing freely you will realise that when your heart is all right, everything is all right.

SUMMARY

• You can work with standard-symbols on small and recurrent issues like pain, stress or tiredness. You just use these symbols when your problem becomes acute and you don't need a problem-symbol.

• You can work with symbol therapy on strengthening positive beliefs in all areas of your life. Formulate a positive statement, picture it and measure how much you believe in it on the scale of belief. Then ask for a healing-symbol to overcome the suffering that comes from your not believing that (name the problem) for the highest good of all beings.

• Symbol therapy can be used to clear away blocks and disharmonies in your chakras. Ask in the usual way for a healing-symbol but visualise your symbol in the chakra you are working with. Let its light and colour expand from there.

–18–
Patterns of improvement with symbol therapy

*W*HEN PEOPLE ARE INEXPERIENCED in self-development they sometimes expect to have a magic breakthrough and to find that their problem has been solved once and for all. Unfortunately it doesn't work like this. Despite the promises of some therapists and despite the enthusiastic reports of some workshop participants, neither any technique nor any form of psychotherapy can offer you this magic breakthrough. Nor can symbol therapy. The reason for this is that the human mind works by building habits. For example, we might have built up a habit of reacting to frustrations with depression or we might have a habit of thinking the worst about ourselves or about members of the opposite sex. People who are happy have developed positive habits like being friendly and loving to themselves and others. Because of this they get a lot of positive feedback which increases their happiness even further.

Everybody has some positive habits and some unwholesome ones. If you want to work on a negative habit you don't need to find out why and when it started because this knowledge – however interesting it might be – will not change the habit. Instead start straight away building a positive habit. A great way of doing this is practising symbol therapy.

Building a new habit doesn't mean that you should try hard to be cheerful when you really feel depressed. That is simply fighting your feelings and is an aggressive act against yourself. We have already discussed why this will never work. All you need to do in order to build a positive habit is to remember your symbol, to trust in it and to do whatever feels right for you in order to solve your problem. With the help of your Higher Consciousness your problem will be transformed rather than suppressed.

With symbol therapy your problem will either get better gradually over time or suddenly from one day to the next. But one thing is sure: your problem will return every now and then. Until your new healthy pattern is deeply established your old negative habit is bound to come back. This is particularly true if you have had a chronic problem.

Imagine that the habit of having your problem is a stream-bed and the water in the stream-bed is your emotions. If you have worked successfully on your problem you will have caused your emotions – the water – to flow into another 'healthier stream-bed' for a while. However, the water will always have a tendency to go back into its old familiar stream-bed and every now and then this will actually happen.

But – and this is the good news – the periods when your problem returns will get shorter and the intervals between these periods will get longer. If you know that there is a certain up and down pattern to your recovery you will feel less frustrated and despondent when your problem comes back. Whenever a symptom comes back, just remember your healing-symbol, breathe it and trust in it.

What time scale can you expect?

If you want to overcome a problem that you have had for many years you can expect to work several months with symbol therapy before you solve it completely. But don't worry, your suffering will be reduced significantly in the first few weeks. In fact, people often experience the most dramatic improvements during the first two weeks of symbol therapy. Then, as they go on working on the different aspects and layers of the same problem with new symbols, the improvements are usually less strong.

If you have had a problem that has lasted many months you can expect to work many weeks on it. And if you have had a problem that has lasted several weeks one two-week period of symbol therapy or even less can be enough to resolve it completely.

Symbol therapy attracts other forms of help

Symbol therapy is not an exclusive method. It can work like a catalyst and trigger other processes that will help you to solve your problem. For example, you might 'coincidentally' find a book that will give you the insights you need or you might 'coincidentally' meet a person who can help you. But you need to actively look out for methods and approaches to solve your problem as well. Physical problems in particular often need some additional treatment.

For those of you who find it difficult to 'get up and do something' about your problems here is another piece of good news. I have observed over and over again that people who have previously just put up with their problems passively suddenly become active in finding solutions for them when they start practising symbol therapy. Their healing-symbol seems to remove the block that had hindered them from actively solving their problem.

John's story can illustrate this point. He was suffering from irritable bladder-syndrome which was very painful and annoying. After he had practised symbol therapy for four weeks his pain had decreased to a bearable level and the times between his need to urinate had become a good deal longer. Still, his problem wasn't completely solved. So he made a list of all kinds of practitioners who he thought might be able to help him. He was determined to try them out one after the other until his problem was solved. This was a very positive development because John had suffered from considerable pain for six years but somehow he hadn't been able to do anything about it. When I asked why he hadn't tried any treatment earlier he shrugged his shoulders and told me that symbol therapy had helped him to develop the real motivation to solve his problem for the first time. John was very satisfied with his results.

Sometimes you will find that you feel strongly drawn to seek help for your problem although this hadn't been your idea when you started symbol therapy. It is good to give in to this urge because the help from your Higher Consciousness can come to you in a multitude of ways and it is important not to have pre-conceived ideas about the way your problem should be solved.

An important source of help is your own ideas. While you are doing symbol therapy it is a good idea to keep a notebook and write your own insights down. Of course, you can never be sure whether these ideas are coming from your Higher Consciousness or from your personal mind. But you need to follow them up anyway. It is no good saying to someone who could help you: *'Thank you very much but I am already working with symbol therapy.'* The little story about Mullah Nasruddin will illustrate this point.

A big flood had engulfed the country and Nasruddin sat on top of a tree well above the water. Nasruddin was a very religious man. He was praying fervently to God to save him and he felt total faith in his heart that this would happen. Suddenly a boat appeared and the people in it offered to pick Nasruddin up. But Nasruddin declined and told them that he was sure that God would save him. The people in the boat tried to convince Nasruddin to join them but finally they gave up and went away. Another boat appeared but Nasruddin declined again. The water rose and rose and finally Nasruddin had to let go of the tree and swim in the water. Again he prayed to God to save him and he still felt optimistic that this would happen. A helicopter appeared but Nasruddin again declined to be picked up. As before he told the people that God would save him. Nasruddin swam for three days and three nights in the water. Then his strength faded and he drowned.

When he appeared in heaven in front of God's throne he was furious. 'I prayed to you three times to save me,' *he said angrily,* 'but you let me drown! Didn't you hear my prayers?'

'I heard your first prayer,' *God said in a mild way,* 'and I sent you a boat. But you declined its help. Then I heard your second prayer and I sent another boat but you declined that one's help. I also heard your third prayer and that time I sent you a helicopter but again you declined its help. What else, Nasruddin, could I have done for you?'

Sometimes new ideas about how to solve your problem will come easily but sometimes they won't. It is possible that you will find yourself agonising over a long-standing problem as usual – even if you do your visualisations painstakingly. Your problem can seem painfully insoluble before you finally find a solution.

If you have an idea about how to solve your problem and it doesn't work, don't give up. Just carry on with your symbol therapy and try to find another solution. Your Higher Consciousness will try to lead you to the solution but it is you who need to take the decisive step of putting your insights into practice.

When my son was a baby he went through a very bad patch. He had one illness after another and at the same time he was teething, which was obviously hurting him a lot. He was whingey and clingy and he was suffering a great deal but his constant crying was driving me mad as well. I practised symbol therapy for both of us and I tried to do as much as I could for him. But nothing was really helping. Suddenly I thought of seeing a homeopathic practitioner and that brought about the breakthrough. The homeopath was so helpful that my son almost immediately returned to being the happy little chap he had been before. Of course, you can ask me why I hadn't thought of homeopathy earlier and to be honest I have asked this question myself. But I can't answer it. All I can say is that I had this idea only after I had started doing symbol therapy and that I was so 'lucky' to find someone who could help me so promptly.

It can be much easier than this. Sometimes my clients report that their symbols seem to have an enormous power to transform their problems at the very moment they think of them. Do you remember my client, Robert, in Chapter 11, who had a serious problem with not being able to be on time? He told me that when he thought of his healing-symbol he almost always managed to be on time against all the odds. He found that really uncanny.

Kate had a loving relationship with her partner but they had sexual problems. To their dismay the passion they had once enjoyed had more or less dried up. When Kate practised her symbol it helped them to rekindle their love-life in just the way they wanted. Of course Kate's partner was as pleased with her practice as she was.

Another way improvement can come about is that your whole situation can change so that your initial problem becomes irrelevant. This happened to Monica, a friend of mine. She had major problems with her ex-boyfriend because she often saw him at places where they had been together before they separated. She didn't want to see him but she didn't want to stop going to these places either. Then something amazing happened. After she had done symbol therapy for four weeks her boyfriend moved to another town.

Of course we can argue about whether his move was because of Monica's symbol therapy. It certainly wouldn't have been ethical for Monica to have wished for her ex-boyfriend to move away in order to get him out of her way. But Monica hadn't wished for this. She had simply hoped that she would gain confidence through her practice. However, when her ex-boyfriend had moved away she was completely released from her problem by this unexpectedly thorough solution.

You will find that it is actually *never* possible to link the solving of your problem directly to the practice of your symbol therapy beyond any doubt. Who can say absolutely why you suddenly feel so much better? And who knows why you had the idea of attending a management seminar and got so much out of it? On the deepest level you will find that symbol therapy is similar to every other method that brings genuine healing – a mystery.

Because it is such a mystery, people sometimes find it hard to acknowledge the effects of symbol therapy. Like Ellen (from the Introduction) they say: *'Yes, I feel better but I don't believe it is because of symbol therapy.'* Or they say: *'Yes, my problem has been solved but it was the shiatsu-practitioner who helped me.'*

This attitude can be a problem because it can discourage you from using symbol therapy again when you have another area which needs improvement.

The help of your Higher Consciousness can only come to you as a gift. All you have to do is to be open to this gift, be grateful for it and use it. This approach demands a certain humility and the acknowledgement that we are not completely in control.

SUMMARY

• No approach, including symbol therapy, can give you a magical breakthrough which solves your problem once and for all. Relapses are part of overcoming your problem but they will be less and less severe and less and less frequent. The human mind likes to create habits and many of our problems are just 'bad' habits. Symbol therapy is an excellent tool for establishing deep positive habits.

• A problem you have had for many years can take several months to be completely resolved with symbol therapy. A problem that has lasted several months can take several weeks to overcome and a problem that has lasted several weeks can be completely resolved in a few days.

• Symbol therapy is not an exclusive method. It can work as a catalyst to attract other sources of help. It is important to follow up these sources of help and you will often find that you have more motivation to do that than you had before.

• Sometimes your whole life-situation can change in such a way that your initial problem becomes irrelevant.

• On its deepest level symbol therapy is a mystery. It will be impossible to link the solving of your problem directly to the practice of symbol therapy beyond any doubt.

−19−
The ultimate
healing-symbol

*Y*OU MIGHT ALREADY HAVE guessed it – the ultimate healing-symbol is your Higher Consciousness itself. There is really no separation between the symbol and what it stands for. The way your Higher Consciousness appears to you really epitomises its full power, compassion and wisdom. In other words, your Higher Consciousness and its symbol are the same and through visualising an image or a symbol of your Higher Consciousness you can directly take in its good qualities.

You can work with the healing-symbol of your Higher Consciousness for any kind of stress or irritation you may encounter in the course of your day and for which you don't have any specific healing-symbol. The symbol of your Higher Consciousness might not take away your bad feelings immediately but it will alleviate your suffering and help you to find better solutions for any problem you might have.

The symbol of your Higher Consciousness can be used in exactly the same way as you use your other healing-symbols. You visualise it in your heart and you breathe its good qualities and bright colour out into your body and into the world.

Using the symbol of your Higher Consciousness will help you in particular with one kind of suffering that no treatment, no kind of psychotherapy and no other symbols will be able to alleviate. It is the suffering that stems from the fact that we are separated from our Higher Consciousness – the suffering of not being in touch with the truth that our most real and deepest nature is our Higher Consciousness and always has been.

Even if we live in the best of all circumstances – with a fantastic career, the best of all partners, as much money as we want and whatever else is important to us – in the back of our mind we know that we will lose it all one day. Even worse, we might lose it at any moment. Our family might die today in a car accident, or tomorrow we might be sacked from our job. No matter how hard we try to ignore this knowledge – there is no real security to be found in this world, anywhere!

Another problem that we share with almost every human being is that nothing can completely satisfy us for long. Even if our deepest wishes are fulfilled it is unlikely that the thrill of this fulfilment will last longer than a few months or years. After that time we will have become used to our new situation and our deep-seated dissatisfaction will resurface and ask for 'more' and 'better'.

Most of us are not fully aware of these kinds of problems because we are so used to them. It's the way we always have been – and we always will be unless we sincerely embark on a spiritual path. But when we don't realise that we are suffering from this 'spiritual illness' of never being able to be completely satisfied for long, we tend to project our inner restlessness and deep-seated anxiety on to our partners, on to our jobs or on to our other life-circumstances. We want to have a perfect partner or we want to find a way of life which will satisfy us completely. But we don't realise that no human condition can give us what we long for most deeply and most intensely, the recognition that we are one with our Higher Consciousness, that we already possess infinite love, happiness and wisdom and that these are independent of any kind of external condition.

If you practise using your Higher Consciousness as a symbol it will not lead you to the complete realisation of your true nature in a matter of weeks or months. But this practice can support you greatly on your spiritual path. If you don't have a spiritual path yet the symbol of your Higher Consciousness can help you to find one.

There are many different spiritual paths to suit the different needs and characters of different people. But all genuine spiritual paths have some qualities in common.

A true spiritual path will above all help us to discover the qualities of our heart, which is both the doorway to and the seat of our Higher Consciousness. Such a path will help us to be more loving and compassionate in a genuine way and teach us the wisdom to realise our true nature. Healing, clairvoyance and many kinds of extraordinary experiences can be side-effects as we develop but it is the realisation of the boundless love of our Higher Consciousness which ultimately matters.

A spiritual path that can genuinely help us in this development will make us feel good about ourselves and at the same time it will make us feel humble. If we follow a religion or spiritual path that tells us that we are intrinsically bad we will never have the chance to recognise that our deepest nature is not bad but on the contrary contains all the qualities of our Higher Consciousness.

However if we follow a spiritual path which feeds our pride and gives us a sense of superiority we will achieve nothing either. The recognition of our Higher Consciousness has nothing to do with having a lot of ideas about how 'great' we are. This kind of self-conceit is completely superfluous when we realise that we *are* pure love and wisdom. In this state we are so happy that we have only one wish and that is to help others.

An emphasis on helping others is the third quality of a genuine spiritual path. Notice whether helping others plays an important part in the religion or path of your choice. Only if there is as much emphasis on help-ing others as there is on helping yourself are you on a genuine path.

SUMMARY

• The ultimate healing-symbol is the symbol of your Higher Consciousness itself.

• You can use the healing-symbol of your Higher Consciousness for any stress and irritation you may encounter in the course of your day and for which you don't have a specific healing-symbol already.

• You can work with the symbol of your Higher Consciousness in exactly the same way as you work with your other healing-symbols. You visualise it in your heart and breathe out its colour and good qualities.

• Working with the symbol of your Higher Consciousness will not make you enlightened within a matter of months but it can lead you on a genuine spiritual path or support you on the one you are already on.

–20–
Practising
symbol therapy
for others

*T*HE BETTER AND THE happier you feel in yourself,
the more you will realise that you can't be fully
happy as long as there are people around you who are
still suffering. If your loved ones are unhappy you will
suffer with them to some extent and generally speaking
people who are unhappy are difficult to be with. Their
frustration and negativity will have a direct effect on you
because on a deep level we are not as separate from each
other as we would like to be. The realisation that you
can't cut yourself off completely from the suffering and
negativity of others can have two effects.

On the one hand you can try to put up your
defences. You can try to ignore the suffering of others
and become critical of people who are negative. If you
know about psychic protection you can put a protective
shield of coloured light around yourself and close your
chakras.

There is nothing wrong with putting up your defences except that they don't change the fact that you still can't be fully happy as long as people are suffering around you. True happiness can only arise when we are open and carefree, when there is no need any more to build walls around ourselves and to take protective measures. Deep happiness happens exactly at the moment when all need for self-protection disappears.

Think about the happiest moments in your life. Were you trying to protect yourself? Were you trying to fence yourself off from other people? Probably not. Most likely these happy moments were at times when you were completely open and unguarded as in the happy embrace of a new lover or in the ecstatic experience of some beautiful aspect of nature or work of art.

This is a real dilemma. On the one hand we can only be genuinely happy when we are open, unguarded and vulnerable but on the other hand the negativity of others affects us much more when we are unprotected.

Luckily there is a way out of this dilemma. There is a way we can be completely open but protected from harm at the same time. This way of being safe, even though we are open, is to have compassion for those who are suffering and those who are negative. When we see their suffering we wish them the best from the bottom of our heart. In other words, the way to be genuinely happy in the face of unhappy negative people is to love them.

To love negative people and to be compassionate towards them is highly demanding and many people may think it impossible. Still, if you are searching for deep happiness there is no other way. And it is less difficult than you think. You can try it now! Think about somebody who has really hurt you and made you angry. When you get a picture of them, say inwardly: *'Although I still don't like what you did and I still want you to change your behaviour, I wish from the bottom of my heart that both you and I find true love and happiness.'*

If you really mean what you have just said, you will find that you immediately feel better, stronger and more peaceful. If you can't always feel this kind of love yet, it is still good to know the direction that the deep happiness we all wish for lies in.

There is something else that can help us to be more loving and compassionate towards negative difficult people. This is maintaining the right distance from them. It is so much easier to be compassionate towards someone negative when they are a little further away from us. And we always have choices about how close we allow other people to get to us.

Of course, it is important that as well as feeling love for others, we must also express our love for them and help them with their problems. In fact, as we start to feel more and more happy and at peace with ourselves, helping others becomes a natural reflex. We just can't help it. It is the nature of true happiness that it wants to expand and include everybody. True happiness is like the sun. When it is shining it sends its light and warmth to everybody without discrimination. So in order to become a genuinely helpful person we need first of all to sort ourselves out and become happy and content. Then we will naturally experience the urge to pass this happiness on to others. One way of doing this is to practise symbol therapy for them. There are several ways we can do this.

1. THE PERSON WHO NEEDS HELP ALREADY PRACTISES SYMBOL THERAPY

You can help this person by practising their symbol for them as well. You need to ask them which healing-symbol they've received from their Higher Consciousness and listen carefully to their description of it. As you already know, the colour is particularly important. Then you need to visualise the person you want to help in front of you and see or sense *their* healing-symbol in *their* heart. When you breathe out you visualise the colour of the symbol billowing out from their heart and filling their body, their aura and their whole surroundings. You do this for two minutes twice a day for two weeks, as you would with your own symbol. Start by telling the person in your mind:

> *'I wish from the bottom of my heart that you find true happiness in all areas of your life.'*

When you do symbol therapy for others it also benefits yourself. It can give you the satisfaction of being able to help the other person and often you will find that you then understand them more. It can also be deeply comforting to yourself and help you to stop worrying about the other person because you can suddenly see the whole problem from a higher perspective.

The baby boy of a woman I knew developed an incurable disease and his mother was half dead with worry. I taught her how to practise symbol therapy for little Thomas and the first thing that happened was that she worried less because she could suddenly see Thomas' illness from a higher perspective. Her trust in God strengthened through this deep crisis and she was more able to let go. My husband and I joined her in her effort to practise symbol therapy for her baby and to the joy of all of us Thomas' condition improved so rapidly that it amazed his doctors.

2. The person who needs help doesn't practise symbol therapy but is happy for you to do it for them

In this case you need to clarify precisely what suffering this person wants to overcome. As you already know the precise definition of the problem is very important. Then you need to ask your own Higher Consciousness for a healing-symbol for them. Ask in the following way:

> **'Higher Consciousness, can you please give me a healing-symbol for** (name of person) **that will help her/him to overcome their suffering from feeling** (name the problem), **for the highest good of all beings.'**

For example, if your sister is very upset with your mother you could ask: *'Dear Krishna, can you please give me a healing-symbol for Sarah that will help her to over-come her suffering from feeling upset about our mother for the highest good of all beings.'*

Next you need to practise the healing-symbol as I have described in point 1.

3. THE PERSON WHO NEEDS HELP HASN'T GIVEN THEIR CONSENT FOR YOU TO PRACTISE SYMBOL THERAPY ON THEIR BEHALF

In some cases it is impossible to get people to consent to your doing symbol therapy for them. There might be no opportunity to talk to them about their personal prob-lems or they might think that symbol therapy is a bit weird. You can still practise symbol therapy for them in the way it is described in point 2 but you need to be care-ful not to impose your own ideas on them.

Let's assume that your husband doesn't talk a lot. You wish that the communication in your marriage was better but you can't even talk about this problem to him. It wouldn't be ethical to ask for a symbol for your husband to overcome his suffering from not talking. Perhaps he is quite satisfied as he is and doesn't want to talk more. In a case like this it would be better to ask for a symbol for *yourself* to overcome *your* suffering from the lack of communication in your marriage. It can be intriguing to see what kind of solution your Higher Consciousness comes up with because it might well involve your husband starting to talk more.

When you do symbol therapy for yourself it can have a powerful effect on other people who are involved in your problem and it can change them in mysterious ways. But it is important to note that this change does not come about through your secret manipulation but through the doing of your Higher Consciousness which always works in the best interest of everybody concerned.

If you want to do symbol therapy on behalf of children under the age of puberty you can define their problem in whatever way feels right for you and then you can ask for a healing-symbol for them from your Higher Consciousness. Then you practise with this symbol as described in point 1. When your children reach the age of eleven or twelve it is best to have their consent if you want to work on their behalf in a specific way. If you don't have their consent you must be careful not to impose your ideas on them as I have described.

Another beautiful option is to teach your children the symbol therapy method and help them to receive their own healing-symbols. If your children like this method it will provide them with an invaluable source of help once they reach the difficult years of puberty and adolescence.

SUMMARY

• The way to feel happy in the presence of difficult and unhappy people is to wish them well but also to keep the right distance from them.

• You can practise symbol therapy for other people in the following ways:

1. If the person in need practises symbol therapy you can practise their healing-symbol for them.

2. If the person in need doesn't practise symbol therapy you need their consent before you ask for a healing-symbol on their behalf and practise it for them. Ask in the following way: 'Higher Consciousness, can you please give me a healing-symbol for (name of person) that will help them to overcome their suffering from feeling (name the problem) for the highest good of all beings.'

3. If you have no consent from the person you can still practise symbol therapy for them but you need to be careful not to impose your ideas on them.

• Before you start visualising the healing-symbol in the heart of the other person tell them in your mind: 'I wish from the bottom of my heart that you find true happiness in all areas of your life.'

−21−
Specific problems with symbol therapy and how to solve them

You are not getting much improvement from practising your healing-symbol

*I*T HAS BEEN VERY rare for people to report to me that they only get a little improvement from symbol therapy. In most of these cases they have not defined their problem in the proper way. But the correct definition of your problem is crucial for symbol therapy to work. The more you can pinpoint the core of your problem the better. If you feel you are not getting the results you expected try to define your problem in another way and ask for a new healing-symbol.

If you find it difficult to define the core of your problem you can ask your Higher Consciousness for help. Say inwardly or aloud:

'Higher Consciousness, please show me the core of my problem.'

Usually you will receive an answer intuitively in the next few days. Then you can ask for a new healing-symbol and try again.

Sometimes people resist the idea of looking for other kinds of help. They might want 'to test' symbol therapy and therefore they avoid any other kind of help in order to see if symbol therapy really works on its own. But it is necessary to be open to other kinds of help and to try them out. If you have a physical problem, for example, symbol therapy can't replace medical treatment. But it can help you to find a good doctor or practitioner. It can also help you to find the motivation and determination to look for something or someone who can help you. If you suddenly think of searching the internet for a solution to your problem don't dismiss this idea – do it! You need to try to solve your problem actively. Your Higher Consciousness will help you and guide you but it is you who needs to put things into practice.

Sometimes people have strong preconceptions about how their problem should be solved and these can become an obstacle.

Sandra had learnt about symbol therapy at one of the talks I gave. She wanted to try the method to work on the 'block' she felt in her lower abdomen. She told me that she had developed a 'fat stomach' a few months earlier and this was really bothering her. Sandra was a therapist herself and she thought that her block was probably caused by suppressed emotions of some kind. She had already done some work in this direction and she started doing symbol therapy with the idea that it would clear away more of the suppressed emotions which were causing the block. She did indeed cry about some long-forgotten grief and this felt good to her but what really helped her 'fat stomach' was something completely different. Sandra told me that she liked the idea that symbol therapy could lead her to a book that would help her. So she followed her intuition that her problem possibly had to do with the onset of the menopause and she picked up a book about this. She read that women of her age are very likely to develop a rounded abdomen. But far from being a nuisance the fat-cells which develop at the onset of the menopause are very healthy and help to reduce symptoms such as hot flushes. Now Sandra, who loves to live in a natural way, is reconciled to her stomach. As you can see, it was very good that Sandra was able let go of her pre-conceived ideas about how her problem should have been solved.

Another reason for poor results with symbol therapy can be that you haven't practised your healing-symbol for long enough. Some people stop doing their symbol if they don't get results in a matter of a few days or they stop as soon as they feel a little better. But if you have had a long-standing problem two weeks are the absolute minimum to produce significant and lasting results.

Sometimes people work with healing-symbols which don't have a beautiful colour or an appealing form. In my experience these symbols are far less effective. You need to relax and ask your Higher Consciousness for a more beautiful healing-symbol.

For some people it is difficult to breathe the colour and the qualities of their healing-symbol *in a loving way* because they hate their symptoms so much.

If this problem applies to you spend some time on loving yourself as a whole being. Think about a moment in your life when you really loved someone and direct this kind of love to yourself. Talk to yourself as you would talk to a beloved child or friend and develop a compassionate heart towards your problems and limitations. These problems are a part of you and it will hurt if you just want to cut them out. Your difficult emotions and physical illnesses or whatever else is bothering you are like sad children who have been mis-treated. They need your love and *gentle* firmness. If you hate them they will just become worse in 'their behaviour' which means that your symptoms will get stronger. Remember, there is nothing better in the whole wide world for healing and improving problems than understanding and wise love.

Your healing-symbol changes of its own accord or you feel the desire to change it

Sometimes a client comes back to me and says that their healing-symbol has changed of its own accord or that they have changed it themselves. In these cases they don't get good results. So firstly you mustn't change your healing-symbol yourself. Even if you feel you want to be an artist and make the colours and the shape of your symbol more beautiful, you mustn't do it! Don't change the colours and don't change the form. Instead, make sure that the healing-symbol you pick in the first place is one that you feel really positive about. After that it shouldn't be changed in any way. If you really feel you want to change it you must ask your Higher Consciousness. Your Higher Consciousness is always the highest authority in symbol therapy and you need to refer to it if you have any doubts. However, don't keep asking for new symbols because your transformative process will be hindered by frequent changes. Two weeks with one symbol is always best.

If your healing-symbol changes of its own accord the same principle applies. Keep visualising your symbol in exactly the form and the colour it was given to you by your Higher Consciousness, even if it is difficult to do this. If your symbol changes or disintegrates relax for a moment and then call it to mind in its original form. You don't need to 'see' every detail. It is enough just to think about your symbol or to sense it as long as it is in its original form.

If your symbol keeps changing you can make a drawing of it and instead of visualising it you can look at your drawing. This always works!

SUMMARY

• If you are not getting much improvement from practising your healing-symbol check the definition of your problem and redefine it if necessary. Check whether your healing-symbol has a beautiful form and colour and ask for a new symbol if this isn't the case. Breathe the qualities of your symbol in a loving way. If this is difficult practise loving yourself in general. Practise your healing-symbol for the required full two-week period. Be active in the process and access any form of help you can think of.

• Always practise your healing-symbol in precisely the form and colour that your Higher Consciousness gave it to you. If this is difficult, relax every time your symbol seems to change and then try to visualise it in its original form. If that doesn't work make a drawing of your symbol and look at the drawing instead of visualising your symbol.

• Don't change your healing-symbol yourself. If you really want another symbol before your two-week period is up you must ask your Higher Consciousness.

The complete practice of symbol therapy

*I*F YOU HAVE COME this far, you now know everything that is necessary to practise symbol therapy success-fully. It's time for you to try the method out. I wish you the best of luck.

PART 1: PREPARATION

- Define your problem as precisely as you can in the form of: *'My suffering from feeling . . .'*
- Measure on a scale from zero to ten how much on average you are suffering from your problem. Zero is no suffering at all, five is a good deal of suffering, and ten is utter desperation.

PART 2: RECEIVING YOUR SYMBOLS
IN DEEP RELAXATION

- Sit or lie down as comfortably as possible and undo all tight clothing. You can put your hands on your stomach to feel the movement of your breathing. Every time you breathe in you feel your hands rise slightly and every time you breathe out you feel your hands fall slightly. Let yourself fall into the outbreath and relax your whole being.

• You are now going on a journey through your whole body. Start with your feet. Bring your awareness into your feet and feel inside your feet. Let all tensions fall away with your outbreath. Now feel into your lower legs and let all tensions fall away with your outbreath. And now do the same with your thighs . . . your abdomen . . . your stomach . . . your chest . . . your shoulders . . . your arms . . . your neck . . . your face . . . your whole head. Your whole being is now wonderfully relaxed – enjoy that feeling.

• And now you sink even more deeply into relaxation and as I count from one to ten you see yourself going down a stairway towards a beautiful and secure place. As I say each number take one step down – sinking deeper and deeper into relaxation:

one . . .

two . . . deeper and deeper . . .

three . . .

four . . . deeper still . . .

five . . .

six . . .

seven . . . deeper . . .

eight . . . and deeper . . .

nine . . .

ten.

- You have now arrived at your beautiful place and you are completely safe here. Find somewhere to make yourself comfortable.
- You are now ready to contact your Higher Consciousness. This is the part of yourself that is completely loving and wise and already knows the answer to all your questions. At the same time it is outside yourself and you share it with everybody else. Your personal Higher Consciousness is also the Higher Consciousness of the whole universe. You can imagine it as a living shimmering light or as an angelic being surrounded by brilliant light or as the central figure of the religion you follow.
- See and feel your Higher Consciousness coming nearer to you. You can feel how its beams of love and light surround you and care for you and you can sense yourself become more loving and joyful when you are touched by the loving and wise presence of your Higher Consciousness. Your Higher Consciousness is a symbol of the unfoldment of your highest potential. To move towards it and finally unite with it is both your ultimate task and your goal in life. Doing this will bring you the kind of joy and happiness which doesn't depend on outer conditions and which can't be taken away from you.
- See your Higher Consciousness on top of a

mountain and ask it to show you a path, a
track or a road leading towards the mountain
top.

- When you see or sense this path ask your Higher
Consciousness: *'Can you please show me where I
am on this path?'*

- When you have received the answer remember
that it doesn't matter whether you are still down
in the valley or whether you are already half-way
up the mountain. All that matters is that you are
moving towards your Higher Consciousness and
that you are unfolding its wonderful qualities.

- Ask your Higher Consciousness to show you
what you are doing on your life-path when you
experience your problem. For example, you may
be straying from your path, walking on the spot
or going downhill. Whatever is shown to you,
don't judge yourself. Ask your Higher
Consciousness in the following way: *'Can you
please show me what I am doing on my life-path
when I suffer from feeling (name the problem)?'*

- When you have received an answer thank your
Higher Consciousness.

- Ask your Higher Consciousness to show you a
healing-symbol to overcome your problem. You
may be shown one or several symbols and you
should pick the one which feels best for you. It
needs to have a beautiful form and colour. Ask in
the following way: *'Higher Consciousness, can you
please give me a healing-symbol to overcome my
suffering from feeling (name the problem) for the*

highest good of all beings.'
- Thank your Higher Consciousness for your healing-symbol.
- Ask your Higher Consciousness for your problem-symbol. This will show you the state of your suffering at the moment. Your problem-symbol will be less beautiful than your healing-symbol. Ask in the following way: *'Higher Consciousness, can you please give me a problem-symbol that shows my current state of suffering from feeling (name the problem).'*
- Thank your Higher Consciousness for its help.
- Tell yourself: *'I always love myself deeply with all my problems and weaknesses and I especially love myself with my suffering from feeling (name the problem).'*
- Remember your healing-symbol and see or sense it in the vast openness of your heart in the middle of your chest.
- Start to breathe out the colour and the good qualities of your healing-symbol. While you breathe out, radiate the colour and the positive qualities of your healing-symbol throughout your whole body and beyond its boundaries into your aura and into the world. If other people are involved in your problem breathe the colour to them as well. If you have a physical problem breathe the colour mainly to the part of your body which needs healing. Breathe the colour of your symbol with all your love and with all your best wishes. Remember, everything changes best

in the light of love. When you breathe in just relax into the positive feeling that comes from seeing or feeling your healing-symbol in your heart. Then exhale its positive qualities again. Do this for two minutes.

• When you are ready, come back into the room.

PART 3: DAILY PRACTICE

• Over the course of the next two weeks see and feel your healing-symbol in your heart and exhale its positive qualities with its colour as described above. Do this for two minutes twice a day and also when your problem becomes acute. Before you start breathing your healing-symbol tell yourself: '*I always love myself deeply with all my problems and weaknesses and I especially love myself with my suffering from feeling (name the problem)*'.

• Visualise your healing-symbol in exactly the form and colour your Higher Consciousness has shown it to you. Don't allow the symbol to change of its own accord and don't change it yourself.

• Be on the look-out for all kinds of insights, whatever source they might come from and write them down in a notebook. Don't be fixated on a particular outcome to your problem but be open to solutions you haven't thought of before. Be active in the process and don't turn down any help in no matter what form it comes to you.

- After two weeks ask your Higher Consciousness to show you your problem-symbol – the symbol that shows you the current state of your suffering. It will very likely have changed for the better. Also ask yourself how much you are still suffering on the scale from zero to ten. Your number will probably be down by at least two points.
- If your problem hasn't been resolved satisfactorily after two weeks you will have arrived at a deeper level or at a different aspect of your problem and you need to ask your Higher Consciousness for a new healing-symbol. If possible ask for a healing-symbol for a different aspect of your problem but keep your initial (but changing) problem-symbol. When your problem-symbol has changed into something really positive and beautiful your problem is solved.

–23–
Passing
symbol therapy
on to others

WOULD YOU LIKE TO pass symbol therapy on to your friends? Would you like to use symbol therapy in your psychotherapeutic practice or would you like to teach this method in evening classes and workshops? You can – you have my explicit permission to do this. There is only one little catch and that is that you have to pass a test. Don't worry, the test is very easy. Before you start to pass on symbol therapy to others I want you to have at least two real personal successes with this method. 'Real' success means that you have practised symbol therapy on two personal issues in exactly the way I have described in this book and that you subjectively classify your results as a success. You should score not more than a one or a two on the scale of suffering and your problem-symbol should have transformed into something really beautiful. With your own success in the back of your mind you will be an empathic counsellor who radiates genuine optimism and you will be a teacher who is able to inspire your students.

It is my deep wish that as many people as possible benefit from symbol therapy and if you feel inspired by this method you are heartily invited to support this aim. In my vision I see people all over the globe solving their debilitating and crippling problems. I see them happier and stronger and in deeper contact with their Higher Consciousness. Tiny sparks of light grow stronger, they grow together and spread. If we are happier as individuals we will influence our whole environment in a positive way. We will bring peace and happiness into our families, to our work-places, to our communities and finally to the whole world. It is a grand aim but we have to start with ourselves.

When you pass symbol therapy on to others don't change the method. Even the smallest details are important. Use and teach the method in exactly the way I have taught it to you in this book. Every now and then I have had clients who tried to 'improve' the method but so far it has never worked out. It is fine to produce audio-cassettes for personal use but I don't want you to produce audio-cassettes and sell them. When you use symbol therapy in your psychotherapeutic practice please make your clients aware of this book and explain to them that symbol therapy is a self-help method which they can use on their own when they are ready.

Study-groups and self-help groups are great ways for practising symbol therapy. Self-help groups are very empowering because they give their participants the additional boost of confidence that comes from the joy of being able to help themselves.

You can start a self-help group by just meeting with one friend. I am sure that after only a short time your work will attract some more friends who want to find out how you are suddenly able to solve one problem in your life after another.

Here are some suggestions for running a self-help group:

- Rotate the leadership of the group every time you meet.
- Use the book or a tape to guide you through the practice in order to receive new symbols.
- Share your experiences with symbol therapy and listen to each other but give advice only if someone explicitly asks for it.
- If you have difficulties with the method refer to this book. But if you can't solve your problem you can write to me and I will do what I can to help you.

May all your problems be resolved. May you awaken your loving heart. May you be happy. I wish you the best of luck!

Index